You Can't Outrun Your Fork

*How to Break the Cycle of Feeling Sick & Tired
and Transition to a Healthier Life, Naturally*

Dr. Anya F. Szigeti, DC, DABCI, MBA

Copyright © 2020 DR. ANYA F. SZIGETI, DC, MBA
All Rights Reserved. Printed in the U.S.A.

All rights reserved. This book or any portion thereof may not be reproduced or used in any manner whatsoever without the express written permission of the publisher except by a reviewer, who may quote brief passages and/or show brief video clips in a review.

Disclaimer: The Publisher and the Author make no representation or warranties with respect to the accuracy or completeness of the contents of this work and specifically disclaim all warranties of fitness for a particular purpose. No warranty may be created or extended by sales or promotional materials. The advice and strategies contained herein may not be suitable for every situation. This work is sold with the understanding that the Publisher is not engaged in rendering legal, accounting or other professional services. If professional assistance is required, the services of a competent professional person should be sought. Neither the Publisher nor the Author shall be liable for damages arising therefrom. The fact that an organization or website is referred to in this work as citation and/or potential source of further information does not mean that the Author or the Publisher endorses the information, the organization or website may provide or recommendations it may make. Further, readers should be aware that internet websites listed in this work may have changed or disappeared between when this work was written and when it is read.

Ordering Information: Quantity sales. Special discounts are available on quantity purchases by corporations, associations, and others. For details, contact the publisher at the address above. Orders by U.S. trade bookstores and wholesalers.
Please contact: info@twopennypublishing.com | TwoPennyPublishing.com

FIRST EDITION
ISBN: 978-1-950995-23-3
Also available in eBook.

For more information about Dr. Anya Szigeti or to book her for your next event or media interview, please contact her via email at: Youcantoutrunyourfork@gmail.com

Healthcare Disclaimer: The information, including but not limited to, text, graphics, images and other material contained in this book are for informational purposes only. The purpose of this book is to promote broad consumer understanding and knowledge of various health topics. It is not intended to be a substitute for professional medical advice, diagnosis or treatment. Always seek the advice of your physician or other qualified healthcare provider with any questions you may have regarding a medical condition or treatment and before undertaking a new health care regimen, and never disregard professional medical advice or delay in seeking it because of something you have read in this book.

This book is written in honor and memory of my mother, Karen, who inspired me to be curious, explore, think outside the box, push the limits, and always ask "why."

CONTENTS

About Dr. Anya	9
Introduction	13

PART 1

Part 1 — Let's Get Started!

Chapter 1 – What Is the Best Diet for Me?	23
Chapter 2 – Is Fat Good for Me?	33
Chapter 3 – What Are the Benefits of Alkaline Foods?	37
Chapter 4 – What Are Healthy Lifestyle Recommendations?	43
Chapter 5 – What Should I Avoid?	47
Chapter 6 – You Can Do It	57

PART 2

Part 2 — Let's Get Cooking!

Chapter 7 –	Great Beginnings	59
Chapter 8 –	Bring on the Veggies	76
Chapter 9 –	More for the Carnivore	104
Chapter 10 –	Dips, Snacks, & Apps	130
Chapter 11 –	Sweetness	140
Chapter 12 –	Beverages	150
Chapter 13 –	For Our Furry Family Members	156

PART 3

Part 3 — Let's Get Healthy!

Chapter 14 –	Shopping, Stocking, Prepping, & Cooking	158
Chapter 15 –	Budget-Friendly Produce Shopping Guides	166
Chapter 16 –	Dr. Anya's Quick Get Healthy List	169

References	171

ACKNOWLEDGMENTS

thank you

Thank you to my taste testers:

Zoltan
Daddy H
Lisa & Nick
Mylo
Beka & Devin
Brook & Aaron
Erica & Karl, Dom & Pierce
Gyula & Alexandra

Thank you for contributing to my story:

My family
Bethany
Dr. Bill
Zoltan
Ambily
Holly
Andrew
Steve

Thank you for proofreading my drafts:

Daddy H
Erica
Holly
Dr. Sarah Kelly
Dr. Bill Kleber
Beka
Zoltan
Bethany
Dr. Michelle D. Jourdan
Dr. Brett Wisnewski

Thank you for inspiring me to write this book and tell my story:

Dr. Derek Schramm
Zoltan Szigeti
Dr. Mark Hyman

ABOUT DR. ANYA

I graduated from the United States Coast Guard Academy with a Bachelor of Science in Mechanical Engineering and I earned my Master of Business Administration from Grantham University. My doctorate is in Chiropractic Medicine with a certification in Acupuncture from the National University of Health Sciences. I completed the 300-hour coursework for the post-doctorate diplomate program in Internal Medicine, Diplomate of the American Board of Chiropractic Internists (DABCI) and passed the two National Board Examinations.

A Chiropractic Internist is a doctor with the tools and training to diagnose a broad spectrum of internal conditions in addition to those of the neuromusculoskeletal system along with education on utilizing natural treatment options. These doctors are not only trained in medical diagnostics, but also employ more alternative and cutting-edge testing to create patient customized natural treatment plans. As a result, many of my patients, who were initially deemed "challenging" or even "hopeless" by the medical community, are now thriving under my care.

The significant difference with my approach is a time-honored method of "detective" work to determine the root cause of health issues. Then, I use nutrition to replace dysfunction and illness with normal body function and health. My treatment plans are generally less about giving something to control or mask symptoms, and more about finding and correcting the source of the disease. The job of a Chiropractic Internist is to search and reveal not only what is going on, but also to answer the question, "why is this happening?" and then design a plan to fix it.

Through my education and experiences, I am trained to think differently. I am uniquely suited to understand the anatomy, physiology, and biochemistry of the human body. This includes how external factors, like the food you eat, the air you breathe, the quality and quantity of your sleep, your stress response, trauma, injuries, and medications or supplements you take all affect your body, for better or for worse.

I treat people, not symptoms. My patients seek out my care for a wide variety of conditions and health concerns. A few common concerns they have are chronic pain, depression, anxiety, environmental toxicity, insomnia, and fatigue.

Women's health concerns include:
- Amenorrhea
- Dysmenorrhea
- PMS/PMDD
- Fibrocystic breast disease
- Infertility
- Menopause symptoms
- Polycystic ovary syndrome (PCOS)
- Urinary tract infection (UTI)
- Uterine fibroids
- Yeast infections
- Hormonal imbalances

Gastrointestinal conditions include:
- Abdominal pain
- Constipation
- Diarrhea
- Heartburn (GERD)
- Food allergies/sensitivities/intolerance
- Gas
- Bloating
- Inflammatory bowel disease:
  - Crohn's
  - Ulcerative Colitis
- Intestinal permeability syndrome/leaky gut
- Irritable bowel syndrome
- Ulcers

Endocrine disorders:
- Adrenal insufficiency
- Metabolic syndrome
- Thyroid disorder
- Healthy weight management
- Autoimmune diseases including:
  - Chronic fatigue syndrome (CFS)
  - Lupus (SLE)
  - Multiple sclerosis (MS)
  - Rheumatoid arthritis
- Thyroid dysfunction
  - Grave's disease
  - Hashimoto thyroiditis

Musculoskeletal conditions:
- Arthritis
- Chronic muscle and joint pain
- Inflammation
- Osteoporosis
- Cardiovascular concerns like:
- Congestive heart failure
- Heart disease
- High cholesterol
- Hypertension
- Palpitations

Neurological dysfunctions like:
- Alzheimer's disease
- Bells' palsy
- Headaches and migraines
- Muscle weakness
- Neuropathy
- Parkinson's disease
- Poor concentration
- Decreased cognitive function

Dermatological concerns including:
- Acne
- Eczema
- Dermatitis
- Fungal infection
- Psoriasis
- Rashes
- Itching

INTRODUCTION

You picked up this book for a reason. Maybe you are looking for guidance on how to live a healthy life, or how to prepare nutritious foods. Maybe you are sick and tired of feeling sick and tired, or possibly you just liked the title. Regardless of the reason, this guidebook is sure to feed your curiosity with wellness facts, provide suggestions with healthy living recommendations, and of course, fill your belly with tasty and delicious recipes. Every day, I help my patients live a healthier life by guiding them to make many of these small dietary and lifestyle adjustments.

This is the guidebook that I wish I had during my health journey. I wrote this book to dispel the misconception that as long as you exercise, you don't have to worry about what you eat and drink. I learned this lesson the hard way. By sharing my struggles, frustrations, and lessons learned, I hope it will educate and inspire you to make the best decisions for your health. This book is for you, and I am excited about the positive changes you will experience in your life when you start to incorporate my suggestions into your daily regime.

Why Should I Care About What I Eat?

When analyzing something, I always like to start with a "why." As a child, I am sure I annoyed my parents with my constant questions. I recall my father being very patient with me. One evening when I was a young child, we were lying underneath the family car while he explained the basics of an automobile engine. For as long as I can remember, my mind always tries to understand what is going on beneath the surface, whether it is an automobile or the human body. One question has stood out to me for years and continues to resurface, "Why should I care about what I eat?"

The fact is, we have to care. Although, I did not care for a long time. I exercised often, so I felt that I could eat and drink whatever my heart desired. But I was very wrong. Maybe you also feel like you don't need to eat healthy because you can exercise more or take supplements. But you can't out-exercise or out-supplement a poor diet, and therefore, you really can't outrun your fork!

Did you know that the incidence of death and disease from lifestyle and dietary choices are increasing exponentially? The sad truth is the incidence of diseases continues to increase daily, even though the cost of developing drugs and surgical procedures to combat these diseases is astronomical. This drives the costs of healthcare sky-high, while chronic diseases plague millions.

Common diseases, like heart disease, cancer, and diabetes were almost non-existent 100 years ago; now they are the leading killers in America. The Center for Disease Control, CDC, reports 6 in 10 Americans suffer from at least one chronic disease. A myriad of other prevalent health conditions that are connected to our poor dietary and lifestyle choices is also increasing. Some of these include infertility, arthritis, autoimmune diseases, ulcers, allergies, learning disabilities, ADHD/ADD, autism, mental illness including anxiety and depression, digestive disorders, obesity, osteoporosis, Alzheimer's, abnormal aging, and chronic fatigue. [6, 7, 12, 28, 37, 39, 40, 46, 48, 51, 52, 57, 59, 61, 66, 68, 70, 72, 73, 74, 83, 84, 87]

We are getting sicker every day, and our current healthcare model is flawed. It has failed many of my patients who have chronic physical and mental illnesses. The latest pandemic to plague us, COVID-19, should serve as a clear call to action to address and resolve underlying conditions like diabetes, heart disease, and cancer. Mortality rates for those suffering from one of these chronic diseases are 5 – 10 times higher when compared to a COVID-19 patient who does not have a pre-existing condition. Obesity, which is also rampant in America, increases the mortality rate three times versus a non-obese patient. Research shows a direct correlation with the consumption of refined white sugar and carbohydrates leading to various brain disorders, including dementia, ADHD, anxiety, depression, and epilepsy according to Neurologist David Perlmutter, MD, author of *Grain Brain*. There is hope for those who take steps towards change. You don't have to live your life this way anymore!

> **"These recipes, along with lifestyle modification and nutraceuticals, have worked amazingly well for me and my patients. I am fascinated by and thoroughly enjoy teaching others about the importance of what and how we should eat, along with the health impacts on our body's biochemistry.
> I am excited to share them with you!"**
>
> ~Dr. Anya Szigeti

Welcome to my recipe collection that I gathered during my struggle with weight, illness, injury, poor dietary, and lifestyle choices. These recipes have been refined through research during my doctorate and post-doctorate education in Chiropractic Medicine, Acupuncture, Internal Disorders, and Nutrition.

The beauty of these recipes is that they contain ingredients commonly found in most of our kitchens and pantries. The majority of the recipes have suggestions and are designed to be flexible to accommodate food allergies, sensitivities, intolerances, and preferences. They will also encourage you to utilize local organic produce and meats. I choose to support local organic farmers, which will aid my local economy and benefit our environment for generations to come.

If this is not an option for you, the ingredients can easily be found and purchased online through amazing companies and in many national chain stores like Costco and Whole Foods. In the appendix, I've included an entire reference guide to stores, cookware recommendations, refrigerator and pantry stocking suggestions, to help get you started. Also included within these recipes are some fantastic ingredients that may be new to you, and since variety is the spice of life, experiment and enjoy this culinary journey!

Zoltan, my husband, is my devoted taste tester. He is one of the most direct and honest people I know, and I love that about him. He is not afraid to tell me when he doesn't like something. When his mother asked him about my cooking, he did not hesitate to tell her about one of my cooking disasters when we were first dating. He reminds me that he still proposed and married me even after serving him the dreaded "garlic chicken."

During that time, I traveled a lot for work so I opted for simple meals that made a lot of leftovers. One of my go-to dishes was chicken in the slow cooker with a few cloves of garlic and some other herbs. I used to purchase pre-peeled garlic cloves, until I watched a documentary on how they were peeled and on this particular day I had a container of them that were almost going bad. Now, if you use garlic often, you know that when they start to go bad, the odor becomes quite potent. I placed the remainder of the container, probably 3-4 times what I would have normally used, into the slow cooker with the chicken, other herbs, and left it for the day. That night, my home smelled of delicious garlic, and I was excited about dinner. I served healthy portions to each of us and watched as my beloved took his first bite. The expression on his face changed as he slowly chewed his dinner. After a few bites, he turned to me and stated that he couldn't finish his meal. I too, was overwhelmed with garlic flavor and was embarrassed about the meal I prepared.

Needless to say, the memory was burned into my husband's memory! And of course, this is the meal that he mentioned to his mother when she asked if I cooked for him. As you experiment with new foods, there will be dishes that you or your family do not enjoy. This is normal, but please try a few new dishes or ingredients each week. Welcome what you learn from this book into your lifestyle at a pace that is comfortable and sustainable. Health is a lifelong journey!

My Story – Why I Began to Care About What I Ate

There was trouble from the start. As a child, I recall having family dinner every night. My mother cooked at home, and we rarely ate at restaurants. A typical meal was meat, vegetables, pasta, rice, bread, or another type of processed carbohydrates. If I knew then what I know now, I would have encouraged my family to skip the processed carbohydrates. The main reason is that several of my family members had symptoms of thyroid disorders. Consuming gluten and processed carbohydrates can wreak havoc on your thyroid function. While in college at the United States Coast Guard Academy and onboard ships during my deployments, I had little control over my food choices. Honestly, I did not understand the relationship between nutrition and my health.

In my early 20s, while on active duty overseas and traveling home from my duty shift, in Nassau, Bahamas, I was in a severe car accident. My car was totaled, and I was left on the side of the road with severe neck and back injuries. The first car to stop asked me if I was okay and if I would like a beer. Now the rules on drinking and driving are a little different in the Bahamas than in America. For the locals, the rule for drinking and driving is, "don't spill." Regardless, I declined the offer for a beer, and they allowed me to use their cell phone to call my co-workers. My doctors told me to hang up my running shoes, and after a few months of being in a back and neck brace, I began believing my running days were over. As a result, I became depressed, made poor dietary and lifestyle choices, and decided that if it came in a box and needed a microwave, it was for me.

Within a few months, I gained over thirty pounds. I did not have the energy to exercise, and even if I attempted to, the pain from my injuries stopped me. To deal with the pain, I began drinking, and my hobbies were reduced to binge-watching TV. This caused me to become even more depressed, and I started down a vicious spiral. Over time I became fed up with being fat, exhausted, depressed, and feeling like crap. I wanted to change my mindset. Through education and the dietary and lifestyle modifications that I will share in this book, I got off the couch, lost the excess weight, proved the doctors wrong, and started to train for endurance events.

In my late 20s and early 30s, I began to have unexplained digestive problems. The doctors I saw at the time were unable to find a diagnosis, so they told me I had irritable bowel syndrome. For me, "syndrome" is code for, "we do not know what is wrong with you, we don't have a surgical procedure or drug to prescribe for it, so there is nothing we can do for you." After doing some research, I decided to eliminate the most common food allergens from my diet to see if they were the cause of my symptoms.

For a few months, I removed these items from my diet: gluten, dairy, eggs, nuts, shellfish, soy, fish, alcohol, and caffeine. The results surprised me as I found that caffeine increased the frequency of my bowel movements, which was not a good thing since they were moving too quickly already! I also found that gluten recreated the bloating, stabbing abdominal pain, and rapid emptying of my bowels. I felt like I was in a fog and was unable to focus or think clearly when I ate gluten. I switched to a "gluten-free lifestyle," but unfortunately, at that time, this included a lot of processed foods and sugars. Yes, I avoided what I thought was the problem, gluten. Still, I was adding in processed and genetically modified (GMO) corn, soy, and other products that can cause serious health issues including inflammation and leaky gut. I knew nothing about cross-reactive foods, which can cause similar issues; and I knew nothing about leaky gut, which is often caused by a combination of an unhealthy diet, stress, consuming gluten, and gluten cross-reactive foods.

Furthermore, I did not know that this leaky gut, if left unchecked, could result in systemic inflammation and trigger an autoimmune disease process. These ailments would linger below the surface and haunt me for years. Initially, changing my diet by going gluten-free provided me with increased energy and, as a result, allowed me the ability to train for and complete two Ironman triathlons and more than nineteen marathon and ultra-marathon races. I began to see the connection between nutrition, lifestyle, and health.

In the beginning, driven by a dream of becoming a "Marathon Maniac," I found three marathons within three months. I signed up for all of them, and convinced my friend, Holly, to join me. Our motto was slow and steady; somewhere along the way, the term "wogging" came about, which is a combination of walking and jogging. I imagine that we looked like two giraffes galloping along as we are both pushing 6' tall.

> "You know all those things you've always wanted to do? You should go do them!"
>
> ~ Unknown

Holly needs to write a book capturing the events of her incredible life. She was always slender and active, and therefore, like me, she felt that she never needed to be concerned with what she ate or drank. Her first major health scare came at the age of 42, after the birth of her second son. She was breastfeeding and noticed a lump in her breast. The doctors initially waived it off as dense breast tissue, but she knew something was not right. Luckily, she had friends who were doctors, and they pushed to get her all the tests she needed to determine what was really going on. The diagnosis was grim, aggressive breast cancer, but she didn't let that get her down. She underwent a radical double mastectomy. As a result of her diagnosis, Holly has altered her diet and lifestyle to include more fruits and vegetables and less sugar. She tries religiously to follow "all of Dr. Anya's recommendations" so she can continue to be an endurance athlete and an amazing mom to her two boys.

We all have our "marathon" or that distance which pushes us beyond our comfort zone. It may be a walk around the block or completing forty Ironman distance events in forty days. Mine evolved as I completed one distance race; I looked up to the next distance to see if I could push myself, train and finish it. In my opinion, completing a sports event of any distance is a great accomplishment!

> "Never, never, never give up."
>
> ~ Winston Churchill

Completing a triathlon is a unique achievement in that there are three different sports to train for along with the transition between each of these events. And you have to keep track of all that gear! I easily spent a year training for my Ironman Triathlon and used shorter multi-sport events as part of my training regimen. After I finished my first Ironman Triathlon, I felt pretty accomplished. I swam 2.4 miles, cycled 112 miles through beautiful Mt. Tremblant, Canada, ran 26.2 miles, and woke up the next morning ready to take on the world. One of my training buddies, Andrew, brought me back to earth with a simple statement, "Anyone can complete an Ironman. If you finish two, now that is really something because you know exactly what to expect the second time around." And just like that, the seed was planted for Ironman #2.

> "I always did something I was a little not ready to do. I think that's how you grow. When there's that moment of, 'wow, I'm not really sure I can do this,' and you push through those moments, that's when you have a breakthrough."
>
> ~ Marissa Mayer, CEO of Yahoo

The weather was beautiful in Cabo the week before my second Ironman Triathlon. The day before the race, a Category 4 Hurricane hit Mexico, south of Cabo, which created tumultuous seas. The undertow was so strong that the race organizers stationed volunteers at the swim exit to pull people out of the ocean. Due to a recent shoulder injury resulting from a bicycle accident in Hungary the month prior, I was unable to lift my arm over my head. A few weeks before the race, I started to train for swimming with the breaststroke versus freestyle. I swam the full 2.4 miles breaststroke and then was pulled out of the raging ocean by the volunteers. After the swim, my shoulder was in a lot of pain, but I pushed through because I still had 112 miles to cycle and 26.2 miles to run. As the temperature rose, my hydration status decreased. For the first time in my life, I got a cramp in my quadriceps while pushing up one of the final climbs of the cycling portion of the race. Just as soon as that cramp subsided, I looked down in horror as my other quadriceps was rippling like it had a snake inside; I was getting a cramp in my other quadriceps. That was the most painful climb of my cycling history. The temperature was in the 90s with high humidity, and I was climbing over 7,500 feet of elevation on my bicycle.

As I started on the run portion of the Ironman, my shoulder started to really hurt. A few sections of the run were loops, and I ran next to an orthopedic surgeon for a short distance. I shared with the surgeon about my accident, and he almost stopped running and exclaimed, "You shouldn't be running this race!"

> "The only disability in life is a bad attitude."
>
> ~ Scott Hamilton, a double amputee

Sadly, as the marathon portion continued, the pain in my shoulder increased. I tucked my arm into my shirt, creating a makeshift sling. At every rest stop, I grabbed some ice and stuffed it in my shirt. The heat in Mexico did not allow the ice to last long, but it temporarily numbed the pain. I lost count of the number of times I thought about giving up. No one would judge me for doing so. But I still had determination deep in my soul that kept me pressing on. I kept thinking, "pain is temporary."

> "The one who struggles hasn't quit."
>
> ~ Race Sign from Raleigh Rock & Roll Marathon

I thought about my mother and her suffering from cancer. She would describe the pain she felt, and I knew the pain I was currently experiencing was nothing compared to the pain she went through. This drove me to keep pressing on, walking and jogging, walking and jogging, until I could hear and see the finish-line in the distance. Behind me, I could hear vehicles that were picking up runners who were not going to make it to the finish-line before the time cut off. This ignited a fire deep within me as I did not want the dreaded DNF (did not finish) to accompany my name for this race. I dug deeper within myself and pushed myself further than I knew I could go.

In true Holly and Anya fashion, we had befriended the race announcer, Steve, at a bar the day prior, so he and Holly were on high alert waiting for me at the finish line. Holly had faith in me that I would complete this race. I stumbled down the final stretch, heard Steve announcing my arrival, and finished just under the 17-hour cut off time. That race was the hardest physical challenge I have ever experienced in my life. Little did I know that it was equipping me with determination and perseverance to fight a different round of battles coming my way with a lot more at stake.

Endurance training has taught me many lessons. One that sincerely stands out for me is learning to listen to my body. This is critical with any level of physical activity as there is a fine line between discomfort and doing damage to your body. You need to listen and learn the signals that your body is sharing with you, indicating that it is at the end of its limit for that training session or race. Otherwise, you may become injured, which may prevent you from reaching your goals or the finish line. I carried this skill over to my diet, lifestyle, and particularly anything that affected my digestion. I began to listen to my body and heed the warning signs that foods or beverages did not agree with me. I also learned how much sleep my body needs and stress management techniques that work for me. Unfortunately, I did not learn my lesson soon enough.

My second punch came a few years later in my late 30s. This was when I learned that even though I raced hundreds of races, my poor dietary and lifestyle choices finally caught up with me, and the truth sank in, I really can't outrun my fork!

After leaving the U.S. Coast Guard, I was offered a medical device sales position and was excited about this opportunity. As I progressed in my career, I was promoted to Regional Sales

Director and was rewarded with a larger territory. This meant more travel, more stress, and less time for my health. I found myself making serious compromises resulting in unhealthy dietary and lifestyle choices. You think I would have learned my lesson already, but no! Stressed and exhausted, I went to my doctor to see if something was going on. I was diagnosed with an autoimmune disease, Hashimoto's Thyroiditis. My primary care provider told me that we would wait until the disease progressed further and then medicate me for the rest of my life. Unhappy with this "solution," I searched for an alternative treatment plan. Thankfully, I was connected with a holistic doctor in Colorado, Dr. Bill, who helped me modify my diet and lifestyle and ultimately halt and reverse my autoimmune disease. This further solidified my belief in nutrition as the cornerstone of our health.

> "Life isn't about waiting for the storm to pass. It's about learning how to dance in the rain..."
>
> ~ Vivian Greene

As a result, I decided to quit my high-stress corporate job. I went to chiropractic school and completed the coursework for two post-doctorate diplomates in Internal Disorders and Nutrition, to become someone who could help others heal naturally! The more I learned about autoimmune disease pathology, the more I understood my disease was likely triggered years before I felt like something was wrong. The repeated cycle of an unhealthy diet and a high-stress lifestyle created the perfect breeding ground for the disease to progress undetected for years until symptoms presented. Even though it is beneficial to our bodies, exercise can also be a source of stress, and exercising for longer than an hour at a time depresses our immune system. So, not only did my endurance training fail to prevent disease, it may have been a contributing factor. After completing medical school, I created my practice, Back to Health Functional Medicine, driven by my suffering from a chronic disease, not finding good solutions with traditional medical providers, and wanting to offer patients better options.

I am now in control of my health, and I manage my weight primarily through nutrition. I have shifted my exercise routines to more focused, nurturing activities like bodyweight HIIT workouts, yoga, swimming, cycling, jogging, and walking while my body continues to heal itself. I feel empowered and better than I have in decades!

> "If you do not step forward, you'll always be in the same place."
>
> ~ Unknown

Through my health journeys, I learned we are not alone in our struggles. I hope to build a community that is a judgment-free zone of healing, nurturing, and support while we all battle our own health concerns. I am honored to be your guide and mentor through this process.

Are you sick and tired of feeling sick and tired? I've been there too! You don't have to live life like this, because we are meant to thrive, not merely survive! I was able to make lasting changes that improved my health, halt and reverse my autoimmune disease process, and increase my energy levels. If it sounds too good to be true, buckle up, and get ready. I'll show you how you can easily make these changes in your life today and get you back on your path to health!

> "Don't Quit. Every difficulty is an opportunity in disguise."
>
> ~ Unknown

What is Different Between This Guidebook & a Cookbook?

Instead of blindly following a recipe and purchasing ingredients you may never use again, this guidebook will teach you how to select the healthiest food options and combine them to make endless healthy, nutritious, and delicious recipes! Get creative and use what is fresh, local, and in-season to make these recipes your own. Feel free to substitute and experiment. If you create something fabulous, please share by emailing me at: youcantoutrunyourfork@gmail.com for an opportunity to be showcased in future special editions!

My grandmother was the epitome of class and elegance. She was also an amazing hostess, cook, and baker. I recall watching her work in the kitchen as a child, amazed by the ease, grace, and perfection with which she created her dishes. I inherited my love of cooking from her, but I did not acquire the perfectionism that often accompanies baking. There is a precision required when measuring and mixing the ingredients for baking, similar to that of a chemist. My mother was a free spirit and an artist. While I am a perfectionist with the majority of the aspects of my life, cooking is one area where my creative, artistic side shines through. I've strived to create recipes in which your creative side can also blossom.

Recipes are passed down from mother to daughter, grandparent to grandchild, mother-in-law to daughter-in-law, sister to sister, and friend to friend. The goal of this book is to encourage you to prepare and cook plant-based meals with ingredients that are local, fresh, and organic, and to understand why it is important to do so rather than blindly following a recipe. Recipes are simply included for a starting point, guidance, and suggestion.

> "Let thy food be thy medicine."
>
> ~Hippocrates

As with any major changes you make to your diet and lifestyle, be sure to consult with your physician before making any significant modifications. The recommendations and suggestions in this book are generalized, and more specific guidance may be required depending on your biochemical makeup and individual health history.

> "The doctor of the future will give no medicine,
> but will interest his patients in the care of the human frame,
> in diet, and in the cause and prevention of disease."
>
> ~ Thomas Edison

PART 1

LET'S GET STARTED!

IN THIS PART:

What Is the Best Diet for Me?
Is Fat Good for Me?
What Are the Benefits of Alkaline Foods?
What Are Healthy Lifestyle Recommendations?
What Should I Avoid?
You Can Do It!

Your body is a temple! Therefore, you should feed it the best fuel you can buy. Always use raw, organic ingredients, including spices, nuts, maple syrup, and honey. Avoid conventional, non-organic, and/or genetically modified organism (GMO) foods. They do not have the healing properties nor the nutritional value of their organic counterpart. Furthermore, they may contain other substances that are damaging to your body.[16, 17, 18, 70, 72, 73, 74]

> "Strive for progress, not perfection. The small steps you make each day have the largest impact on your overall long-term health."
>
> ~Dr. Anya Szigeti

1

What is the Best Diet for Me?

> "Fall in love with taking care of your body."
>
> ~Unknown

I often get asked, "what is the best diet for me?" The simple answer is to eat a diet consisting of a wide variety of whole foods, primarily organic vegetables and fruits, whole grains, healthy fats, wild seafood, grass-fed and organic meats. Eat food that comes from the earth and not from a box.
16, 17, 30, 37, 70, 72, 73, 74, 75

In every meal and snack, incorporate:
1. Fiber
2. Protein
3. Healthy fat
4. Something green

One great thing with many vegetables, let's take an avocado, for example, is that it fits every category –fiber, healthy fat, protein, and it is green! I often drizzle some olive oil and sprinkle a little sea salt on half of an avocado for a quick, healthy snack. Another quick, healthy, and easy snack suggestion is raw organic celery sticks with organic nut butter. This snack also fits all four categories. Celery is packed full of fiber and is green; nut butters are healthy fats that contain protein.

Timing is important with nutrition and eating. Many conditions have shown benefits with intermittent fasting where you do not consume calories for a set period of time, typically around 13-16 hours. This is not a new concept as breakfast literally means breaking a "fast," but it has gained popularity recently. If you finish eating dinner around 7 pm, implementing intermittent fasting would mean that you would not consume any calories until after 8 am the next morning. According to Dr. Mark Hyman, this pattern of eating balances blood sugar levels, reduces inflammation, increases antioxidants, stem cell production, mitochondrial repair, bone density, muscle mass, and cognitive function. I've noticed with myself that my "after dinner" and "late-night" eating choices are usually not the healthiest, so I try to avoid eating after I finish dinner.

How much should I eat?

We always tease my dad that he eats until he is 80% full and then stops himself. But, it's actually a great philosophy to visualize your stomach as a tank of gas, and only fill it to 80% capacity. Listen to your body, and it will tell you when it is satisfied. Keep in mind that it's not necessarily the quantity you eat, but rather the quality of what you eat that has the biggest impact on your health. This is the foundation of Functional Nutrition. For example, eating a large salad full of vegetables, including an avocado, nuts, and a healthy dressing may be high in fat and calories, but they are "good and healthy" fats and calories. These are required for proper biochemical reactions in our bodies so it can heal and function at an optimal level. [70, 72, 73, 74]

This 80% rule applies when eating healthy foods, like those highlighted in this book, but does not extrapolate as well to unhealthy foods. For example, let's compare the salad above with a pizza. While you will feel full when you eat pizza, keep in mind that a typical pizza is made with ingredients like gluten, dairy, and tomatoes (a nightshade vegetable that can cause damaging inflammation.) If you ate until you were 80% full of unhealthy foods and ignore the salad, it omits the benefits of the healing foods. Pizza is one of my favorite foods, but now I space out my indulgence once a month versus a few times a week, and I pair it with salad or make sure it is covered with veggies.

"Can I eat too little food?"

Yes, it is possible to not consume enough calories. This puts our body into a starvation state. While in this state, the body stores energy as fat because it senses that soon it might not have enough energy to function. Starvation also puts stress on our bodies, pushing it away from the healing "rest and digest" mode, and into the chronic stress "fight or flight" mode.

"Am I eating too much or too little?"

A great place to start is to record everything you eat and drink. Be sure to include how you feel after you eat and drink something. This way, you can track what you are consuming and learn to listen to your body by documenting how it makes you feel. Sharing this information with your Functional Medicine Physician will help them to make additional recommendations. As part of my initial paperwork, I have all my patients complete a 7-day diet log. This is eye-opening for them, and many of my patients continue to journal and track their food and beverage consumption throughout the course of their care. One patient, who has struggled with weight their entire life, has adopted this as a lifetime habit to keep themselves accountable and has noticed significant improvements in their health, increased energy levels, and healthy weight loss as a result.

What foods should I eat?

Are you confused about the food options available to you? Food industry marketing is often misleading, which adds to the frustration and challenges of eating healthy. Fad diets create unhealthy eating habits, which often result in weight gain. Nutrition is the foundation of health. Exercise is important, but as I've learned many times throughout my life, that regardless of the number of races you complete, no matter how hard you try or how far you go, you can't exercise away poor dietary and lifestyle choices. Therefore, you really can't outrun your fork! An alternative that many people try is using supplements in an attempt to fill in the gaps left behind by their poor diet. This also fails to work properly as you can't out-supplement a poor diet. The quick answer to the initial question is to fill your plate with organic vegetables, fruits, grass-fed and organic meats, seeds, nuts, and other healthy fats. I will explain and expand on all of these later in the book and provide specific recommendations. [70, 72, 73, 74]

Do I have to eat my veggies?

Vegetables are the foundation of a plant-based, whole-food lifestyle and should be a part of every meal and snack. They enrich the body's immune system by supplying critical vitamins, minerals, antioxidants, and phytochemicals which are necessary for biochemical reactions within our body. Vegetables also allow us to heal and repair from injury, detoxify, and support our immune system to function at an optimal level. Non-starchy vegetables and fruits are also excellent sources of beneficial fiber. [70, 72, 73, 74]

> **"Eat foods that God created, not 'foods' created in a lab."**
>
> ~ Dr. Anya Szigeti

"Is there a resource that can help me decide which produce I could purchase non-organic?"

> note — *Chapter 15 shares a produce reference.*

The Environmental Working Group (EWG) is a nonprofit and environmental watchdog organization. They analyze data supplied by the United States Department of Agriculture (USDA) and the Food and Drug Administration (FDA) regarding pesticide residue on our food. Annually they release a "Shopper's Guide to Pesticide in Produce." This contains two lists of the highest "Dirty Dozen" and lowest "Clean Fifteen," levels of pesticides in commercial crops. The EWG's 2020 "Clean Fifteen" list is the fifteen produce items with the lowest levels of pesticide residue.

If cost or availability is an issue, purchase these following items non-organic: avocados, pineapples, onions, sweet peas, eggplants, asparagus, cauliflower, cantaloupe, broccoli, mushrooms, cabbage, honeydew melon, and kiwi. Since there is still pesticide residue present on these produce items, always wash them well before consuming. Be cautious with sweet corn, papaya, and summer squash, including zucchini, as non-organic versions in the US are often genetically modified. Therefore, I recommend purchasing the organic version of these foods.[21]

Dark leafy green vegetables are superstars when it comes to nutrition. They contain powerful antioxidants and vitamins A, C, E, and K which help prevent cellular damage that can cause inflammation. These powerhouses are also great sources of B-vitamins which help our bodies respond to stress in a healthy manner and nourish the nervous system with the anti-inflammatory Omega-3 fatty acids. Spinach is also a potent antioxidant, containing fiber that aids with digestion and reduces fatigue.

The allium family of vegetables offer many health benefits, including onions, leeks, shallots, scallions, garlic, and chives. Garlic is a superstar medicinal food that has been shown to possess antibacterial, antiviral, and antifungal properties, as well as reduce cholesterol and blood pressure. Garlic is also a powerful antioxidant. Onions are a great source of immune-boosting vitamin C, allergy relieving quercetin, and they have anti-inflammatory properties.

Artichokes contain powerful antioxidants that support the liver by enhancing its ability to filter and eliminate toxins, and contain fiber which aids with healthy digestion. They are great sources of potassium, magnesium, and phosphorus; all of these electrolytes are beneficial to our muscles, especially the heart, and therefore, are fantastic for athletes of all levels to incorporate into their diets.

Mushrooms are an immune-modulating and apoptogenic superfood. They have been shown to aid with viral infections, colds, arthritis, asthma, and boost immune system function. Mushrooms are a great source of plant-based protein, fiber, immune-boosting vitamin D, calcium, and the powerful antioxidant selenium. Selenium supports healthy thyroid function and helps prevent damage to our cells and tissues. I ensure that I have my daily dose of organic immune-boosting mushrooms in my morning coffee (page 62).

I have an autoimmune condition called Hashimoto's Thyroiditis, and therefore, I avoid eating raw broccoli and other members of the brassica family of vegetables. Raw brassica vegetables should be avoided by all of us who have a thyroid disorder as they contain substances that are goitrogenic or can cause thyroid goiters. These include broccoli, cabbage, cauliflower, brussels sprouts, kale, and bok choy. The cooked versions provide a multitude of health benefits without negatively affecting thyroid function. Cabbage is antimicrobial and aids in healing the stomach lining and ulcers. Broccoli is anti-inflammatory and an antioxidant; it helps to regulate blood pressure, blood sugar, and increases blood flow. There is a correlation between consuming broccoli and preventing migraines, a reduction in breast cancer risk, and lower cholesterol levels. Brussels sprouts are a potent antioxidant and anti-carcinogenic.

Variety is the spice of life! There are so many fantastic and unique vegetables available. I try to eat the colors of the rainbow every week and recommend for you to do so as well. Each color group has different phytonutrients that benefit our bodies in unique ways, so be sure to branch out. Broaden your horizon and try a new vegetable each week. Some you may not like, but others may surprise you. Be sure to shop your local farmers' markets and purchase organic produce that is in-season as it will have the highest nutrient density.

According to a 2009 study of phytonutrient consumption from data gathered by the National Health and Nutrition Examination Survey, 8 out of 10 Americans are falling short on every color category. Add a variety of colors to your meals by putting berries into your breakfast smoothie and filling a scramble or egg cups with various vegetables. Salads and collard green wraps are great ways to increase vegetable consumption for lunch or light dinners. I like to experiment with different roasted vegetables as additions to our dinners. I've included a plethora of delicious veggie-packed recipes for you to try!

What types of carbohydrates do I need to comsume?

The majority of your carbohydrate intake should be from organic fresh fruits and vegetables. Raw fruits are an excellent source of antioxidants, fiber, vitamins, and minerals. Utilize fruits, ideally organic berries, as your dessert or as a treat and avoid consuming fruit with added sugar. Be cautious with dried fruit due to high sugar and preservative content, unless made at home and then only consume in small quantities. [70, 72, 73, 74]

> "If you are not hungry enough to eat an apple, you're not really hungry."
>
> ~ Michael Pollan, Author of *Food Rules*

Do you move your bowels every day? Fiber is critical for digestive health. It aids with moving the bowels, feeding beneficial gut bacteria, and binds to toxins to prepare them to be eliminated from the body. For women, fiber is especially important because it binds to excess estrogen and allows for its removal through the bowels. Raw vegetables and fruits are excellent sources of fiber. Artichokes have one of the highest-fiber contents of 10 grams! "An apple a day keeps the doctor away," but be sure it is organic and eat the peel because that is where most of the fiber is. The vegetables with the highest fiber content include organic sweet potatoes (with the skin), broccoli, carrots, beets, dark leafy greens like swiss chard and kale, and of course, artichokes. Fruits packed with fiber include organic apples, berries, guava, mango, and oranges. [70, 72, 73, 74]

What type of protein is healthiest for me?

note *Chapter 14 shares a quick reference and shopping guide.*

Did you know that consuming too much of the wrong type of protein can lead to systemic inflammation and increased cancer risks? Anti-inflammatory, plant-based, and grass-fed organic proteins are essential to a healthy diet because they help heal and repair tissues. There are nine amino acids deemed essential because our bodies cannot produce them, so we must obtain them through our diet. Complete sources of amino acids contain the majority of these nine essential amino acids, from plant-based protein foods including quinoa, hemp seeds, and chia seeds. Depending on your individual sensitivities, you may be able to incorporate beans, legumes, and small amounts of organic tofu. Some people find these foods to be inflammatory and cause them digestive issues; if this is the case for you, then it is best to avoid them entirely. [70, 72, 73, 74]

If you choose to eat meat, you want to eat the healthiest meat available. Organic, grass-fed meat is an excellent source of protein, as it contains essential amino acids, essential fatty acids, B-vitamins, iron, and minerals. As we will discuss, conventionally raised meats are inflammatory to our bodies and have large scale detrimental environmental impacts as well. Therefore, eat 100% grass-fed meat, including the fat and organs, as they are an amazing source of B-vitamins, especially vitamin B-12.

Shop from local farmer's markets and look for organic food delivery in your area. Many local farmers utilize organic practices and do not use growth hormones or antibiotics, but may not have the official "organic" designation due to cost restrictions as it is expensive to be designated an "organic" farm. If an animal is given antibiotics for any reason, their milk, eggs, or meat cannot be labeled "certified organic." The Standard American Diet (SAD) contains a large percentage of conventionally raised meat and meat products. Ideally, healthier meat should be consumed in smaller quantities, and even though it may cost a little more than the alternative, if you eat a little less, it will benefit both your wallet and your waistline. [3, 31, 85]

I recommend eating wild-caught, coldwater fish, and seafood. This is another great source of protein, essential fatty acids, amino acids, and iron. In addition, seafood contains iodine, which is required for thyroid hormone production, vitamin D, and vital trace minerals like zinc. The EWG also publishes lists to assist with selecting healthy fish and seafood options. The EWG's "Best Bets" list includes seafood with very high levels of Omega-3, low mercury, and are sustainable. These include salmon, sardines, mussels, rainbow trout, and atlantic mackerel. Secondary good choices include oysters, pollock, and herring. The EWG recommends avoiding king mackerel, marlin, orange roughy, shark, swordfish, and tilefish due to high mercury levels. [20, 21, 22, 49, 77, 86]

Another great resource for seafood is the National Resource Defense Council. They created "The Smart Seafood Buying Guide" available on their website: ***https://www.nrdc.org/stories/smart-seafood-buying-guide***.

This guide recommends five easy steps to select seafood:

1. Think small by consuming smaller fish that are not at the end of the food chain.
2. Buy American raised fish as the FDA regulates our fishing practices, but many countries do not have strict oversight.
3. Diversify your palate as the majority of Americans consume only five types of seafood: shrimp, salmon, canned tuna, tilapia, and pollock. The high demand can cause habitat destruction, harmful fishing tactics, overuse of antibiotics, and overfishing.
4. Eat local – think "boat to fork" like you do "farm to fork." ***LocalCatch.org*** is a great guide to community-supported fisheries near you.
5. Be vigilant and research where you are purchasing your seafood from. Inquire if the seafood offered is sustainably harvested.

Make your own bone broth (page 106). Bone broth is prepared with organic, grass-fed animal bones, simmered for several hours. The slow cooking process releases healing amino acids glycine, proline, and arginine from the bones. Drinking or cooking with bone broth helps support the digestive tract by bringing digestive juices to the gastrointestinal system, reduces joint pain, and repairs damaged tissues. I enjoy drinking bone broth and visualize the healing it is doing while I drink it. My husband, on the other hand, cannot imagine drinking it, but enjoys when I cook rice and quinoa or make soups with bone broth. [3, 70, 72, 73, 74]

Bacon is a controversial food with regard to health. Simply put, healthy versions of bacon are beneficial, while unhealthy versions are not. The key difference is located on the ingredients label. Healthy bacon should include only organic pork and salt. Unhealthy bacon contains dangerous preservatives, nitrates, and nitrites which are converted to carcinogenic compounds called nitrosamines when heated. Therefore, cooking unhealthy bacon converts the preservatives into dangerous cancer-causing compounds. Healthy bacon has a fatty acid profile similar to that of olive oil, and the majority is beneficial oleic acid. Oleic acid has been shown to have a positive effect on cancer, autoimmune, and inflammatory diseases. One serving of bacon contains 37g of protein, B-Vitamins, selenium, phosphorous, iron, magnesium, zinc, and potassium. [67, 78]

SUCCESS STORY

I've known my dear friend, Bethany, her whole life. Her father and my mother grew up around the corner from each other, and our mothers were pregnant with us at the same time. Like me, Bethany was also a good weight and exercised often, so she ate and drank whatever she felt like. At age 37, after being sick, most likely with a viral infection, she was diagnosed with Type 1 Diabetes. After her diagnosis, we discussed changing her diet, which included reducing her intake of sugar and processed foods, and instead incorporating healing, anti-inflammatory foods and more vegetables. I introduced her to bone broth and avocado eggs, both of which she really enjoyed, and these recipes (page 71) are included in this book. Bethany has incorporated many of the dietary and lifestyle recommendations I've made, and as a result, she has noticed a significant improvement in her overall health.

Sadly, I often hear this scenario from my patients, "I was fine, and then one day, I was not." What if the decisions we've made gravely affected our future? What if we could go back? I wish that I could! Unfortunately, we cannot go back in time, but you do have the power to educate yourself and make adjustments to your dietary and lifestyle choices today that will lead you on a path away from disease and towards health. And, even better, you have the instruction manual in your hands.

2

Is Fat Good for Me?

Do you want to have more energy? Fats are used to produce energy and needed in the creation of the membrane around every cell in our body. The goal is to incorporate a small amount of healthy fat into every meal and snack. Healthy fats are anti-inflammatory, minimally processed, rich in Omega-3, monounsaturated, and beneficial for our bodies. When purchasing oils, the label should read "cold-pressed," "expeller pressed," "unrefined," "extra virgin," and "organic."

Other great sources of beneficial Omega-3 fatty acids are sea vegetables, green vegetables, avocados, and most nuts and seeds. Both flaxseeds and chia seeds contain exceptionally high levels of Omega-3 fatty acids. Avocados are particularly beneficial for women to consume during and after pregnancy. They provide key nutrients for fetal development and increase the levels of antioxidants and fatty acids that are passed to the baby via breast milk. Sea vegetables like kelp and seaweed also contain iodine, which is beneficial for regulating thyroid function. [70, 72, 73, 74]

In Hungary, where my husband is from, and many other countries, duck and pork grease are prized as cooking mediums. My husband's mother and aunt save every drop and use them in a variety of dishes. The animal's source is typically from local farms and often from the neighbor down the street who has several ducks, geese, and chickens in their yard. In many countries, they utilize the entire animal, organs, skin, fat, and bones in their meal. Not only is this practice more sustainable and environmentally friendly than just using certain cuts of meat and discarding the rest, as is often done in America, but it also provides you with a plethora of critical nutrients, vitamins, minerals, and healthy fats. Picture using an entire chicken versus just the breasts or thighs. You can cook the entire bird, organs, head, and feet included, making a nutrient-dense soup, retaining the bones to make bone broth. If you have a pet, you can feed them the skin and cartilage (not the bones) mixed in with their food, as long as it was cooked without seasonings. Buying the entire bird costs less per pound, and you can make a lot more food that is more healing and nutrient-rich than just using a certain cut of meat.

My husband likes to tease me by calling me a "coconut head." I utilize coconut oil in my homemade deodorant and whipped body butter, as an oil treatment for my hair and nails, and daily oil pulling for dental health; therefore, I literally smell like a coconut. Coconut oil is an all-around superfood and nutrient powerhouse with a multitude of health benefits and uses. It contains healthy saturated fats that are processed differently than other dietary fats. These medium-chain triglycerides (MCTs) are quickly processed by the liver and encourage the body to burn fat to provide a quick energy source for both the body and the brain. I add it to my morning coffee; recipe included. Coconut oil contains a powerful antimicrobial called lauric acid, which converts to monolaurin in our bodies. These substances have been shown to kill the bacteria staphylococcus aureus and the harmful yeast candida. Coconut oil is also great for our furry family members. I feed our little puppy, Mylo, coconut oil and wipe some on his paws and fur daily. [3, 70, 72, 73, 74]

"I've heard that eating fat is unhealthy; it is bad for my heart, and that I should eat a "low-fat" diet." The Framingham Heart Study is one of the largest and longest-running studies on heart disease and its causation. It started with 5,209 adult subjects in 1948, and is now studying the 4th generation. The director and co-director shared their results, and the information may shock you. The key takeaway is that we have all been misled to believe that saturated fat is not good for us, and therefore, we should switch our diet to eat low-fat foods. The reality is that saturated fat is critical to our health, especially for our brain, and provides our body with energy and cholesterol, which are the building blocks for all of our hormones. So, if you want energy, brainpower, and a positive mood, eat healthy fat.

> **"If you didn't need a pill to get fat, why would you need one to get un-fat?"**
>
> ~ Unknown

How do I cook with healthy fats and oils?

When fat and oils are heated, their chemical composition changes. It is important to match the cooking temperature with the correct oil or fat. Purchase oils packaged with tight-fitting lids in dark glass bottles and avoid plastic bottles. Store oils and fats in a dark, cool location away from the stove, microwave, top of the refrigerator, or other heat sources. [15, 36]

High heat – Refined avocado oil 520°F, refined grass-fed ghee (butter with milk solids removed) 450°F, grass-fed tallow 400°F
Broiling and high-temperature roasting/baking (400°F – Broil)
Sautéing meats (375°F-400°F)

Medium heat – Lard (duck, pork, and bacon fat) 375°F and extra virgin coconut oil 350°F
Medium temperature baking (350°F-375°F)
Sautéing vegetables (300°F-350°F)

Low heat – Extra virgin olive oil 325°F
Low-temperature baking (250°F-325°F)
Finishing on cooked meats and vegetable (no heat)

Best oils for salad dressing (no heat) – Flax, walnut, macadamia, sesame, and olive oils

> "In Framingham, MA, the more saturated fat one ate,
> the more cholesterol one ate, the more calories one ate,
> the lower people's serum cholesterol...
> we found that the people who ate the most cholesterol,
> ate the most saturated fat, ate the most calories weighed the least,
> and were more physically active."
>
> ~ William Castelli, MD, Director, The Framingham Heart Study

Is Fat Good for Me?

> "The diet-heart hypothesis has been repeatedly shown to be wrong, and yet, for complicated reasons of pride, profit, and prejudice, the hypothesis continues to be exploited by scientists, fund-raising enterprises, food companies, and even governmental agencies. The public is being deceived by the greatest health scam of the century."
>
> ~ George Mann, ScD, MD, co-director,
> The Framingham Heart Study

3

What Are the Benefits of Alkaline Foods?

Alkalinity neutralizes acidity. Acidity can lead to oxidative stress, and is one of the leading causes of numerous health issues, including diseases such as cancer. Alkaline diets are connected with several health benefits, including reducing hypertension and stroke risks, reduction in muscle wasting, and improvements in cardiovascular health, memory, and cognition. [71]

My favorite foods for increasing alkalinity are organic avocado, kale, cucumbers, broccoli, spinach, lemons, limes, celery, and bell peppers. Interesting fact: lemons, limes, and other "acidic" citrus fruits actually provide an alkalizing effect when processed in our bodies.

What is Lacto-Fermentation?

My husband teases me that our laundry room should be called the sauerkraut room. When I learned about the benefits of Lacto-fermentation, I immediately started to incorporate it into our diet. My husband and I loved it so much that we were buying large containers each week. The best tasting organic version was pricey. Friends gave us a container of their homemade sauerkraut, and it motivated me to learn how to make my own. After a few attempts, I found a great balance of salt, water, and organic cabbage. The recipe (page 90) is included for you to try!

Lacto-fermentation is a process that turns a simple vegetable into a probiotic, nutrient-dense superfood. The "Lacto" stands for lactobacillus bacteria, not lactose, and is dairy-free. Lacto-fermentation includes only salt, water, and vegetables and is the oldest form of food preservation in the world. The saltwater creates an environment where only lactobacillus bacteria can survive and acts as a preservative, keeping harmful bacteria out. The result is a tasty, healthy, safe vegetable full of gut-friendly beneficial bacteria, and it is preserved, naturally. [87]

There are numerous benefits of consuming lactobacillus in Lacto-fermented foods. Some of these benefits include improved digestion, increased energy production, increased immune system function, clearer skin, and reduction in brain fog, anxiety, depression, and mood swings. [43, 55, 64, 87]

How do I cook with, store, and propagate fresh herbs?

My mother shared with me her love of culture, experiences, and different foods. In college, she spent a year traveling the world, living with different families, and immersing herself in their culture. This desire to explore and learn was ingrained in me from a young age. She encouraged me to try new foods and travel to new places. My travels thus far have taken me to some exotic and intriguing locations, two of which expanded my understanding and appreciation for cooking with fresh herbs. The first country was India, and the second was Hungary.

I traveled with my friend, Ambily, to visit her family and explore the country of India. Standing 5'10" tall, I was an entire head above the majority of the population. This made it easy to see where I was going and also for Ambily to find me in a crowd. Several people stopped me at the train station asking for my autograph as they thought I was a WNBA player. One of our first stops after arriving in the country was to her grandparents' home. Her grandfather spoke fluent English, and I was excited to speak with him. I loved his sense of humor.

Her grandmother was making lunch for us and I noticed that she grabbed a long stick and went outside. My curiosity led me to follow her to see what she was doing. She reached the stick up into a tree and began to knock small branches and leaves off. She gathered them and brought them into the kitchen and put them in our meal. I inquired with Ambily as to what it was, and she told me it was curry leaves. I was astonished as the only curry I had ever seen was the yellowish-orange powder or paste. The chicken curry Ambily's grandmother made was delicious!

This memory was tucked in the back of my head until my husband and I bought our new house. The property had many different trees, shrubs, and plants, which took me a while to identify. One set of trees stood out, and I realized they were curry trees. Now I can make curry dishes with my own curry leaves, and I've included recipes (pages 80, 81, and 115) for you to try as well. Don't worry if you don't have your own curry tree as the powder and paste versions make delicious meals too.

My husband and I try to go to Hungary every year to spend time with his family and friends. The Hungarian language is one of the most difficult languages in the world to learn as it doesn't have roots in any other language. I attempted to learn a few words before my first trip, but my pronunciation was terrible. My in-law's property contained many fruit and nut trees, as well as a massive garden brimming over with vegetables and herbs. My mother-in-law loves to cook, and she is continuously baking or preparing something in the kitchen. Just like my mother, she always has food ready for visitors and never wants you to go a moment feeling hungry. I enjoyed watching her prepare and cook different meals, but I was fascinated when she stuffed a bunch of cucumbers in a jar and set them on the porch in the sun. It never dawned on me until this moment that you could make pickles this way. I honestly just thought of them as something you bought pre-made in the store.

The language barrier made inquiring about the recipe nearly impossible as she did not speak English, and I did not speak Hungarian. My husband translated for us and she agreed to show me how to make the next batch. Using fresh dill from her garden, which I had never seen before outside of a seasoning jar, and cucumbers also from her garden, she created her simple masterpiece. Her days of teaching in the local schools gave her patience, and she lovingly walked me through each step, using non-verbal communication to ensure I understood the process. We expanded our cooking education sessions to include several of my husband's favorite Hungarian dishes as well.

Herbs have long been praised for their medicinal value and their flavoring power. Keeping organic dried herbs on hand is a great alternative, but nothing beats the fresh stuff. Fresh organic herbs are easy to care for houseplants and great garden companions. When utilizing herbs as functional foods, be cautious with heating and cooking herbs as it may reduce their phytochemicals and beneficial healing properties. Avoid microwaving, stir-frying, roasting, or grilling fresh herbs. Ideally, use them as soups or raw as toppings. If you need to use them and do not want to consume them raw, like garlic, for example, add it in the last 5-10 minutes of cooking.[60]

DILL has been used for digestive problems like indigestion, constipation, and gas. I love using fresh dill to make pickles, on top of wild-caught fish like salmon, and in my salad dressing.

GINGER is a potent anti-inflammatory and beneficial for a wide range of conditions, including nausea, digestive issues, motion sickness, arthritis, headaches, colds, flu, and joint and muscle pain. Sliced ginger adds a refreshing tang to infused water or hot tea. I often use freshly grated ginger root in sauces and marinades.

CILANTRO promotes digestive secretions to aid in proper digestion, reduces oxidative stress, and aids in the detoxification pathways within our body. I love to sprinkle fresh cilantro on carnitas and taco dishes as well as use it when making guacamole. I always use the stems and leaves and add them to my salad dressing.

CINNAMON has antibacterial and antifungal properties, and has been shown to aid in blood sugar regulation and enhance immune function. I found that cinnamon is fantastic sprinkled on roasted chicken drumsticks and, of course, delicious in warm beverages.

TURMERIC is a powerful antioxidant that inhibits many harmful enzymes, which allows the body to heal and repair damaged tissues. The anti-inflammatory power stems from the active component, curcumin, and its effectiveness is comparable to that of prescription medications, without the toxic side effects. It can help reduce inflammation associated with indigestion, inflammatory bowel disease, arthritis, cystic fibrosis, autoimmune diseases, and cancer. To aid with the absorption of the bioactive compounds, always consume turmeric with black pepper. I love to use turmeric in soups, sprinkled on meats, and in golden milk.

An oil contained in **BASIL**, called eugenol, inhibits enzymes that create inflammation. Eugenol acts on the same enzyme targeted by Nonsteroidal anti-inflammatory drugs (NSAIDs). I trim the flowers off my fresh basil plants, roughly chop them, and place them into a glass jar covered with organic olive oil. After allowing it to marinate for a few days, I use this basil-infused oil as a salad dressing or drizzled on salmon.

GARLIC is a powerhouse of healing. It contains a wide variety of sulfurous compounds that reduces systemic inflammation and has antiviral and antibacterial properties. Friends tease me that I can't make a meal without incorporating garlic. I often chuckle to myself when I read a recipe that calls for one clove of garlic while I add five or six! Garlic is a staple in my salad dressing, soups, and just about everything I cook.

ROSEMARY has anti-inflammatory, antioxidant, and neuroprotective properties. I love to use fresh rosemary in my salad dressing, and sprinkled on roasted sweet potatoes and salmon during the last few minutes of cooking. Dried rosemary can be tough and rarely softens during cooking. Therefore, I highly recommend buying a rosemary plant.

Propagation of fresh organic herbs is easy to do. Start by trimming the end of fresh herbs stems, remove the bottom leaves, and place them in freshwater. Roots should appear in a few days or weeks, depending on the temperature and type of herb. Be sure to change out the water often and ensure no leaves or debris are in the water, or it will rot. I have had the most success propagating mint and basil. Once the herb shoot makes roots, place them in a pot filled with organic soil mixed with organic compost or plant them in your garden near vegetables as they ward off pests and are beneficial to many plants. For example, basil planted near tomato plants yields a sweeter harvest with fewer pests. Mint helps to ward off aphids but will spread quickly, so I keep my mint in small pots and place them around my garden.[38]

Fresh organic herbs keep well in the refrigerator. Simply trim the stems, remove the bottom leaves, and place in a glass half-filled with water. Again, be sure no leaves or debris are in the water, or it will rot. Cover the herbs with a reusable produce or plastic vegetable bag and change out the water often.

A few suggestions for incorporating fresh organic herbs:

- Use fresh organic mint leaves for tea or infused water with sliced organic ginger root and sliced organic lemons.
- Freeze organic mint leaves in an ice cube tray filled with organic pomegranate or tart cherry juice and add to soda water for a refreshing summer drink.
- Make your own herb-infused organic olive oil by using the flowers, stems, and small leaves of organic basil plants. Roughly chop the fresh organic basil, place in a small wide-mouth jar with a lid, like a mason jar. Add enough organic olive oil to cover the fresh herbs and swirl to ensure they are submerged and place in a cool, dark place. Check the oil a few times a week and give the jar a swirl, adding more oil as needed to ensure herbs remain submerged. The oil will be ready once you can smell the aroma and then simply remove the fresh herbs. You can also make delicious herb-infused oils with fresh rosemary, sage, and thyme. These infused oils are great for salad dressings or finishing drizzles on vegetables and meat dishes.

> **"Grow your health!"**
>
> ~ Dr. Anya Szigeti

4

What Are Healthy Dietary & Lifestyle Recommendations?

> **note:** *Read Chapter 15 for "Dr. Anya's Quick Guide to Health."*

Build your meal around plant-based foods, especially vegetables. Think of meat as a condiment, added to accent a meal instead of the focus of the meal. If you choose to omit meat from your diet, be sure to supplement with B-vitamins and ideally work with a Functional Medicine Physician to identify and resolve any vitamin or mineral deficiencies. [3, 70, 72, 73, 74]

Flavor foods with healing organic spices and herbs (e.g., garlic, ginger, onion, turmeric, and cayenne) and make your own sauces, dips, marinades, and salad dressings (recipes on pages 99, 101, 119, and 132-173). Use raw organic unfiltered apple cider vinegar, with the "mother," which contains beneficial nutrients and bacteria, as a base for salad dressings along with organic olive oil. Apple cider vinegar is an excellent source of beneficial bacteria called probiotics, necessary for healthy digestion and immune system function. In addition, apple cider vinegar can aid in achieving proper stomach acid levels. Healthy stomach acid pH is between 0-1. This helps with digesting and absorbing proteins, vitamins, and minerals, as well as defending against harmful bacteria, viruses, fungus, and other microbes. It reduces systemic inflammation and has shown benefits for a wide range of conditions, including Crohn's disease, colitis, arthritis, diabetes, colds, and the flu. [70, 72, 73, 74]

Snack on organic raw olives, coconut, nuts, and seeds, but be mindful of portion size. These healthy fats also contain protein, fiber, minerals, vitamins, and antioxidants. Ensure they are raw, organic, unseasoned, and unsalted. Walnuts, hemp seeds, chia seeds, and flaxseeds are particularly high in beneficial, anti-inflammatory Omega-3 fatty acids. [70, 72, 73, 74]

Select from organic coconut, olive, and avocado oils when cooking and baking. Utilize refined avocado oil for higher heat, above 400F, while cooking, sautéing, and baking. Refer to the "How Do I cook with Healthy Fats and Oils" section (page 35) for specifics. [70, 72, 73, 74]

Drink lots of fresh filtered water daily. Aim for half your body weight in ounces every day. For example–if you weigh 150 lbs. then you should be drinking 75 ounces of freshwater daily. Infused water is a delicious way to increase hydration. There are several tasty recipes (starting on page 152-153) included in this book. [70, 72, 73, 74]

> "Nothing is impossible. The word itself says 'I'm Possible'!"
> ~ Unknown

If alcohol is consumed, ensure it is organic red or white wine and be mindful of limiting consumption to 1-2 glasses a week. Conventionally raised grapes have high levels of pesticides, and non-organic wine has higher levels of preservatives called sulfites, which can cause negative side effects. Drinking alcohol in excess, more than a few drinks a week, can cause an increase in the production of an inflammatory marker called C-reactive protein. Alcoholic beverages typically contain addictive sugar, leading us to drink more than we planned, cause unhealthy blood sugar spikes and poor dietary choices, give us headaches, and suppress our immune system function. Alcohol destroys our essential gastrointestinal beneficial bacteria, which is a critical part of both of our immune and digestive systems. An imbalance in our microbiome beneficial bacteria can result in a condition called leaky gut, where our gut lining opens, allowing larger particles of foods to penetrate the intestinal barrier, and this activates the immune system, inducing further inflammation, allergies and is a potential trigger in autoimmune disease pathology. [70, 72, 73, 74]

If caffeine is consumed, select organic coffee or green tea without added refined sugar or cow's dairy. Listen to your body and be mindful of caffeine, which can have a hyperactive effect on your digestive system, often leading to digestive and absorption issues. Raw honey can be added if sweetness is desired. Organic nut milk is delicious in coffee. Be mindful to read the labels to ensure there are no additives or preservatives like sodium metabisulfite and/or thickeners like carrageenan, locust bean gum, and gellan gum, if you do not make your own. These preservatives and thickeners can cause inflammation and digestive problems within the body. If using a canned version, ensure the label clearly states "BPA-free." Conventionally grown tea leaves and coffee beans have high levels of pesticides; therefore, always purchase organic versions of these foods, which are high in antioxidants. [70, 72, 73, 74]

I recommend exercising daily. Even a daily 15-minute walk has marvelous health benefits.

Practice yoga, spend time in nature and get some sunshine, read, walk, meditate and set aside time each day for deep conscious breathing. These all aid with calming the response to stress and improving the duration and quality of sleep. [70, 72, 73, 74]

Without rest and under stress, the body cannot heal, repair, and rebuild. There are two nervous systems within our body, and they compete for attention. Only one is active at a time, either – "Rest and Digest" or "Fight or Flight." When you are "fighting" or stressed, your body can not digest its food properly or heal. Even the perception of stress is enough to cause digestive issues. Therefore, it is imperative to learn how to balance the unnatural stress response through natural techniques like meditation, exercise, and deep breathing.

Without proper rest, the body cannot heal. Sleep is the time for our brains to process the events of the day and for our bodies to heal and repair tissue. Rest can boost our memory, reduce inflammation, and control appetite. Most people should aim for 7-8 hours of sleep each night. Be sure to put down your electronic devices at least one, but ideally two hours before bedtime. We are exposing our eyes to "blue lights" from television screens, computers, tablets, and phones delaying the release of melatonin. Melatonin is the hormone which is responsible for healthy sleep patterns. The levels should be highest just before falling asleep and decrease as the night progresses, so you wake alert and ready to embrace the day.

> "It takes 4 weeks for you to notice your body changing, 8 weeks for your friends, and 12 weeks for the rest of the world. Give it 12 weeks. Don't give up!"
>
> ~ Unknown

How can I live without sweets?

Do you have a sweet tooth? Don't worry, I've included many healthy "sweetness" recipes (page 141) in this book. Many of these recipes include cacao. Cacao is a superfood and a rich source of antioxidants, anti-inflammatory flavonols, and anti-aging polyphenols. It contains magnesium, which has calming properties and contains plant compounds to support a focused mind and a positive attitude. I purchase a large bag of raw, organic cacao on Amazon, but if you do not have cacao, you can substitute with 70%+ organic dark baking chocolate powder, which also contains antioxidants and anti-inflammatory compounds.

Two sweeteners are showcased in the recipes contained in this book, honey and maple syrup. Raw organic local honey is rich in healing amino acids, digestive enzymes, and has immune-boosting antiviral properties. Bees gather pollen from flowers to create the honey, and consuming locally created honey can aid in reducing seasonal allergy symptoms. Raw organic maple syrup is loaded with B-vitamins, zinc, and antioxidants. It is immune-boosting and helps to protect our cells and tissues from damage. [70, 72, 73, 74]

Organic berries, including blueberries, raspberries, blackberries, and strawberries, are excellent sources of antioxidants that help reduce damage to our cells and tissues. They also inhibit the enzymes which promote inflammation. The high fiber content of these tasty little nutrient powerhouses is beneficial to the digestive tract, cardiovascular system, and helps to balance blood sugar levels. They are the preferred fruit options due to their positive effect on balancing blood sugar. Other fruits, especially dried fruits, contain up to 10 times the levels of fructose, which is a sugar that can quickly spike and then depress our blood sugar to unhealthy levels, potentially damaging blood vessels. For dessert, I enjoy a bowl of organic berries topped with organic whipped coconut and cacao nibs. [70, 72, 73, 74]

> "No one who fetched their groceries by only walking to the grocery store and then carrying their grocery bags home could carry enough to have significant weight issues. Obesity would not be a problem in a practicing society."
>
> ~ David A. Schramm

5

What Should I Avoid?

> **note** — *See Chapter 14 for Quick Reference Guides*

Did you know that the earth provides us with all the foods we require to nourish and heal our bodies? Therefore, avoid all refined and processed "food" products that are pre-packaged or sold in boxes. Even just fourteen days on an unprocessed food diet has shown a statistically significant loss of body fat and weight.[33]

I compiled a list of the most common questions that my patients ask regarding diet and what to avoid, since you may have similar questions.

> "Refined food accounts for **63%** of the average American's diet."
>
> ~ Dr. Phil Maffetone

"What if my pantry is full of convenient, quick packaged foods, and I often buy less expensive GMO and dairy products, are these okay for me to eat?"

Let's define refined foods, this includes packaged and processed foods. Avoid all refined white sugar, refined white flour, gluten (some examples are wheat, orzo, rye, spelt, bran, germ, semolina, barley, bulgar, cereal, couscous, pasta, muffins, pancakes, waffles, bread, crackers, cookies, cakes, etc.). Avoid all genetically modified "foods" or organisms (GMOs), any "foods" containing preservatives, artificial sweeteners, and/or artificial colors. Also, avoid consuming any products with pasteurized cow's milk or trans-fat. Read the labels of every product before you purchase and consume them. When reading ingredients labels, follow these two simple rules:

1. If you can't pronounce it, don't eat it!
2. If there are more than five ingredients, it's not for you! [70, 72, 73, 74, 85]

"What is the deal with gluten?"

Gluten is used in many baked goods and processed foods; it is essentially the glue that holds the other ingredients together. Gluten is hard for our digestive system to process and can lead to digestive issues, even in people who do not have a specific allergy, intolerance, or sensitivity to gluten. Several foods cause a cross-reactive reaction in people who have a negative reaction to gluten. These include corn, millet, oats, rice, yeast, amaranth, soy, sesame, wine, beer, buckwheat, tapioca, teff, sorghum, quinoa, spelt, hemp, polish wheat, white potatoes, eggs, coffee, chocolate, and every dairy product (even lactose-free and from non-bovine sources).

Eliminating these foods from your diet may improve your skin, mood, digestion, sleep quality, and increase your energy levels. Discussed in detail in the next few paragraphs, avoiding these foods may also reduce your chances of having a leaky gut, which is directly related to an increased risk of activating autoimmune disease processes. [3, 70, 72, 73, 74]

"I do not have an allergy, so why should I avoid gluten?"

Gluten is a mixture of two proteins that give doughs an elastic, fluffy characteristic, essentially holding the ingredients together. One of the proteins, gliadin, can cause a severe autoimmune reaction in people with celiac disease. This causes the absorption mechanisms of the small intestines, called microvilli, to be destroyed by the immune reaction leading to digestive distress and nutrient deficiencies. Also, the immune response from gluten can lead to sinus problems, brain fog, joint pain, blood sugar imbalances, hormonal imbalances, and skin issues.

Gluten has also been linked to leaky gut and systemic inflammation, both of which are considered triggers for autoimmune disease pathology. These symptoms can appear in anyone, even those without the autoimmune disease, celiac. Therefore, it is advisable to speak with your Functional Medicine Physician if you suffer from a chronic or inflammatory disease or have any of these symptoms. [3, 70, 72, 73, 74]

"Is going gluten-free a fad or for real?"

Going gluten-free may seem like an easy step with all the processed foods created by the food industry to profit off this latest trend, but consuming these alternative foods does not address the underlying issues. Many gluten-free products are laden with highly processed, gluten cross-reactive ingredients and sugars to make them appealing and addictive. Instead of reaching for that package of gluten-free cookies, grab an organic apple instead. Fill your plate with foods from the earth, including a wide variety of colorful organic fruits and vegetables, nuts, seeds, grass-fed meats, and wild-caught fish. [3, 70, 72, 73, 74]

"My sister and I can eat the same meal, and afterward, I am bloated and uncomfortable, and she is fine. Why is this?"

Each individual's health status and biochemistry are unique, and as a result, each of us responds differently to consuming the same foods. And this response can change throughout our lifetime. It is influenced by lifestyle and environmental factors like chronic stress, sleep deprivation, dehydration, nutritional deficiencies, digestive disorders, heavy metal toxicity, and infections. Therefore, it is important to listen to what your body is telling you. It will tell you what foods it likes and what it does not. All you have to do is listen and heed the signals. Do not ignore signs like exhaustion, reliance on caffeine, forgetfulness, moodiness, or skin changes. These are not normal and are often signs from our body telling us something is wrong internally.

"How do I know if I have an allergy, intolerance, or sensitivity to certain foods?"

Negative food reactions can occur at any time in our life and can change throughout our life as well. Avoid all known food allergens, intolerances, and sensitivities. Avoid any foods that "do not agree with you." Symptoms of a negative food reaction include: skin irritation, flushing, rash, abdominal bloating, pain, gas, vomiting, upset stomach, changes in bowel movements, sneezing, nasal congestion, coughing, hoarseness, throat itching or tightness, difficulty swallowing, wheezing, shortness of breath, changes in heartbeat, anxiety, feeling of doom, dizziness, loss of consciousness, metallic taste in the mouth, uterine cramping, urinary urgency and/or anaphylaxis.

The eight most common food allergens are eggs, peanuts, tree nuts, fish, shellfish, dairy products, wheat, and soy. If you are experiencing possible symptoms of a negative food reaction, a simple elimination diet can aid you in determining if any of these foods are the causative agent. Your Functional Medicine Physician can order testing to identify exactly what your body is reacting to and guide you through how to perform an elimination diet to identify possible food triggers and negative food reactions. Above all, listen to your body and heed the messages! [3, 59, 70, 72, 73, 74]

"Are there additional foods I should avoid if I have a chronic condition?"

If you are suffering from an inflammatory condition like arthritis, headaches, gout, hypertension, cancer, kidney disease, thyroid disorder, or autoimmune disease, you should avoid a family of vegetables called nightshades. This family includes tomatoes, white potatoes, eggplant, peppers, and tobacco. These vegetables have been shown to lead to inflammation and are high in lectins, which can disrupt metabolism and bind to the stomach lining leading to digestive issues.

"I have heard that a lot of animals used to prepare our food are fed antibiotics. Why is this and how bad is it for my health?"

Conventionally raised (non-organic and non-grass-fed) animals are fed foods that are not natural for them, and this causes them to be sick. The animals are forced to live in crowded facilities, wading in their own feces and urine with diseased and dead animals. As a result, these animals have to be fed antibiotics and growth hormones, which then makes their meat inflaming and damaging to our bodies. The FDA reported in 2014 that the agriculture industry purchased 80% of all the antibiotics sold in America to give to these sick animals.

Two great resources are available to learn more about animal agriculture practices in America and their effects on our health and the environment, Concentrated Animal Feeding Operations (CAFO) and Environmental Working Group (EWG). CAFO provides information about the practices of industrial animal agriculture and the risks to public health and the environment, as well as the mistreatment of the animals on their website: **CAFOthebook.org**. EWG has a guide to meat-related labels, certifications, and best practices for the health-conscious meat eater. EWG's "Meat Eater's Guide to Climate Change and Health" is available on their website: **EWG.org/meateatersguide/eat-smart**.[31]

"I've been told that I should eat more fish; I see wild-caught and farmed fish for sale in my grocery store. What is the difference?"

Farm-raised fish and seafood are often fed an unhealthy diet of genetically modified corn, soy, or vegetable oils. This diet results in fish that are lacking the beneficial Omega 3 oils and are high in the inflammatory Omega 6 oils. Omega-3 fatty acids are plentiful in wild-caught fish. The crowded, unnatural living conditions in which farmed fish are raised are a breeding ground for diseases. Chemicals and antibiotics are used in an attempt to control the diseases, but these toxins spread, poisoning wild populations, and, sadly, negatively affect our ecosystem for generations to come. All this combined makes farmed fish unhealthy for us to consume and just like selecting meat and meat products, you want to consume the healthiest fish possible.[20, 49, 77, 86, 88]

"Can I purchase dips and sauces that are already made?"

Unfortunately, most premade sauces, marinades, dips, and salad dressings are high in refined sugar, refined salt, unhealthy fats, and preservatives. Take control over what you consume! Make your own delicious sauces, dressings, and dips with recipes (pages 99, 101, 119, 132-137) included in this book as a guide. Get creative with what you can find locally or grow in your own garden. You will be able to harness the healing power of herbs to nourish your body and save money too.[33, 70, 72, 73, 74]

> "Take care of your body. It's the only place you have to live."
>
> ~ Jim Rohn

I used to love roasted, salted cashews until I learned that the oils become rancid when heated and release free radicals that are harmful to our bodies. In addition, the seasonings and type of salt used are unhealthy. Therefore, I recommend avoiding roasted, flavored, and/or salted nuts and ideally opt for raw, organic versions.[33, 70, 72, 73, 74]

"I know that smoking and excessive drinking are bad for my health, but how bad is it really?"

Alcohol or tobacco product use alone causes detrimental health risks and increased mortality rates, yet the risks escalate substantially when used together. The risk of developing oral cancer for a smoker or drinker is 6-7 times higher than someone who uses neither. But someone who uses both tobacco products and drinks alcohol, the risk of developing oral cancer increases 300 times! Three hundred times increased cancer risk. Yes, it really is that bad for you, and that is why you should avoid smoking or using any tobacco products and drinking beer or hard liquor.[11, 13, 34, 58, 63, 65, 70, 72, 73, 74, 90]

> "The food you eat can be either the safest and most powerful form of medicine or the slowest form of poison."
>
> ~Ann Wigmore

"What if I cannot find organic produce, are there varying levels of pesticides on different produce items?"

The EWG compiles a list of the highest levels of pesticide residue on our produce items and updates it annually. Therefore, it is best to avoid conventionally grown produce listed on the EWG's 2020 "Dirty Dozen" as they contain the highest levels of pesticides: strawberries, spinach, kale, nectarines, apples, grapes, peaches, cherries, pears, tomatoes, celery, and potatoes. Non-organic hot peppers are treated with neurotoxic pesticides. Always purchase these produce items organic.[18, 22]

 *See Chapter 16 for a quick list.*

Along any journey, there will be bumps in the road. Convenience, taste, and cost are three obstacles that my patients throw back at me when we discuss dietary adjustments. You may be asking, "what if I need to eat some ice cream or a cheeseburger?" Allowing yourself the freedom to indulge is a part of the joy in life. The goal is to space the indulgences out, so they are no longer a daily occurrence. Wherever you are today, work towards an 80%/20% and then a 90%/10% split of healthy foods vs. indulgences. Maybe there is an emotional connection to certain foods. It will take some time to rewire your brain, especially the reward center. Start by rewarding yourself with flowers, a walk in the park, or reading a good book versus a sugary or fatty treat. Contained within these pages are practical solutions to address the common obstacles that may be preventing you from leading a healthier life, like convenience, taste, and cost. Remember to take it one forkful at a time because you can't outrun your fork.

> "We can reverse years of damage to our bodies by deciding to raise our standards for ourselves and then living differently. Old wounds heal, injuries repair, and the whole system improves with just a few changes in what we put into our bodies and how we move them."
>
> ~ Unknown

WHAT IS UNHEALTHY FAT?

"Are certain types of fat detrimental to my health?"

Any form of refined trans or hydrogenated fat or oil is unhealthy and should not be consumed. The Institute of Medicine determined that "there is no safe level of consumption of industrial trans-fat from partially hydrogenated oil." These types of unhealthy fats are often found in margarine, store-bought salad dressings, mayonnaise, tartar sauce, and many other processed foods. Avoid consuming any item with "partially hydrogenated" on the label, like deep-fried and most packaged foods. Here is a shortlist of the most common unhealthy fats to avoid consuming: canola, vegetable, corn, cottonseed, safflower, peanut, soybean, sunflower, and grapeseed oils.[42]

"What is the correlation between unhealthy fats and my health?"

According to the United States Department of Agriculture - Human Nutrition Information Service (USDA-HNIS), during the 1920s-1960s, there was a rapid increase in heart disease. During this time, Americans' consumption of animal fats was replaced with hydrogenated and industrially processed vegetable fats. The great majority of the artery clogs discovered during these heart examinations were from unsaturated fatty acids, which are a direct result of consuming hydrogenated and industrially processed vegetable fats. As a result, margarine eaters have twice the rate of heart disease as butter eaters. Cholesterol is the building block for all our hormones, including neurotransmitters in our brain. Therefore, low-fat diets are correlated with increased rates of suicide, violence, fatigue, depression, and psychological problems.[26, 42, 89]

What are the concerns with eating dairy?

I used to eat frozen sticks of butter as a child, and my dad used to have to take the block of white cheddar cheese away from me. I loved and still love dairy. Yet, during my nutrition education and research for this book, I have learned some scary information behind one of my favorite foods. Conventional (non-organic, non-grass-fed) cow's milk produced in the US is loaded with antibiotics and growth hormones, called recombinant bovine growth hormone (rBGH,) or recombinant bovine somatotropin (rBST,) all of which wreak havoc inside our bodies. This hormone use in dairy cattle has been banned in the EU for decades! The genetically engineered hormone, rBGH/rBST, is injected into cows to increase milk production and has been linked to breast, prostate, and colon cancers in humans. Cows that are treated with rBGH/rBST are more likely to develop mastitis, or udder inflammation, in response to infections that require antibiotics.

The bacteria that cause mastitis are contagious and are easily passed to other cows due to the unsanitary conditions of commercial cattle houses. The antibiotics are excreted into the cow's milk along with blood, pus, and any other toxins the cow is exposed to. The American Cancer Society states the use of rBGH/rBST and antibiotics in conventional cow's milk does increase the incidence of antibiotic-resistant bacteria and raises the concern about the health implications for humans. [2, 23, 62, 82]

Therefore, the majority of the recipes in this book do not contain dairy products, and if they do, it can easily be omitted. If you should choose to consume dairy, it should only be in strict moderation. I still consume dairy, but try to select minimal servings of grass-fed, organic dairy products ideally from non-cow and non-bovine milk sources like goat or sheep's milk, which are closer in composition to that of human breast milk. Therefore, it is less likely to cause a negative food reaction. Nut and seed milk and yogurt are delicious alternatives and easy to make at home.

What are the dangers of eating sugar?

I enjoy a sweet treat as much as the next person, and I used to not read nutrition labels nor pay attention to the sugar content of the food I consumed. The more I've learned about the dangers of refined white sugar, the more I removed it from my diet. As a result, I have noticed that fruits taste sweeter and my palate can appreciate a wider range of flavors, in addition to the numerous health benefits of not consuming refined white sugar.

Instead, I opt for natural sweeteners and fruits. Refined white sugar is not an ingredient in any recipe in this book, and for a good reason, it is dangerous to our health. Natural alternatives which provide sweetness to recipes include raw organic maple syrup, raw organic honey, organic stevia leaf, organic and sulfate-free dried fruits like dates and apricots.

Refined white sugar causes extreme blood sugar swings, which can damage blood vessels. These blood sugar swings also cause you to feel fatigued, moody and cause false hunger leading to unwanted weight gain. Consuming refined white sugar signals our bodies to release stress hormones, which further leads to anxiety and irritability. Over time, eating refined white sugar can lead to obesity, diabetes, premature aging, including cognitive decline, tooth decay, gum disease, dyslipidemia, elevated blood pressure, non-alcoholic fatty liver disease, and heart disease. There is new research showing a connection to cancer risk and elevated blood sugar. [4, 5, 8, 9, 10, 14, 19, 25, 29, 44, 45, 47, 50, 51, 54, 57, 80]

Our gastrointestinal microbiome is a delicate balance of beneficial bacteria and yeast. A strong immune system and healthy diet allow the body to handle a certain level of "bad" bacteria and yeast. But consuming refined white sugar feeds the harmful bacteria and pathogenic yeast, which can lead to a decreased ability to fight disease and cause infections like Small Intestine Bacterial Overgrowth (SIBO) and yeast overgrowth called Candidiasis. Eating refined white sugar leads to deficiencies in critical vitamins and minerals like vitamins A, C, B-12, and chromium. These vitamins and minerals are essential for immune function, energy production, and blood sugar management. [4, 5, 8, 9, 10, 14, 19, 25, 29, 44, 45, 47, 50, 54, 57, 80]

Why is refined white sugar hidden in processed foods? It is good for business!

1. It is cheap.
2. It is addictive, so you will want to buy and consume more.

It terrified me to learn that the average American consumes 57 pounds of added refined white sugar annually. Even worse is that "healthy," "natural," "diet," and "low-fat" foods labeled to be "good" for us contain added refined white sugar either by that name or one of the hundreds of names the food industry has invented to trick us into buying their product. Your safest and healthiest bet is to buy local, fresh, organic produce and make your own meals at home.[81]

> ## "The question is not can you, it's, will you?"
>
> ### ~ Unknown

Did you know that there are currently 61 names for sugar? These include high-fructose corn syrup, cane sugar, cane juice, brown sugar, artificial sweetener, rice syrup, molasses, caramel, and any additive ending in "-ose" like glucose, maltose, or dextrose. Some common products which contain refined sugar include cookies, cakes, pastries, bread, pasta, cereal including granola, crackers, protein bars, protein shakes, premade beverages like vitamin-enriched water, fruit juice, iced tea, chocolate milk, coffee, sports drinks, premade soup, canned fruit, beans, vegetables, dried fruit, "low fat" yogurt, salad dressing, condiments like BBQ sauce, peanut butter, ketchup, tomato, and pasta sauce. [1, 35, 53, 70, 72, 73, 74, 75]

> "Sugar stimulates the brain's reward centers through the neurotransmitter dopamine exactly like other addictive drugs… Foods high in fat and sweets stimulate the release of the body's own opioids (chemicals like morphine) in the brain… Animals and humans experience 'withdrawal' when suddenly cut off from sugar, just like addicts detoxing from drugs."
>
> ~ Dr. Mark Hyman,
> *Food Addiction: Could It Explain Why 70 Percent of America is Fat?*

6

You Can Do It!

You have the power to live a healthy life, and the key lies at the end of your fork. In this lifelong journey, strive for progress, not perfection. Focus on making smart, healthy decisions every day. You don't have to punish yourself or feel guilty if you "cheat." I did it, often, and you will too. It's okay to have a "bad" meal, but let's not make it two in a row. Take a deep breath, hug yourself, and get back on track. Don't feel like you need to deprive yourself of every food you once enjoyed. Educate yourself and decide on a few small changes. The goal is to begin. You took the first step by purchasing this guidebook, and now it is time to place one foot in front of the other down your pathway towards a healthier life. I've been there, and I will walk with you every step of the way. It is easiest to start small, with these two steps, and you will have greater success in the long term:

> "It always seems **impossible** until it's done."
>
> ~ Nelson Mandela

1. Stop buying ultra-refined and processed foods.
2. Start buying organic, whole, plant-based foods.

My #1 weight loss tip is to stop going out to eat, buying food from restaurants, and consuming premade, processed foods. Instead, buy local, in-season, organic, fresh produce, and make your own food at home. This will have the added benefit of supporting your local small businesses and farming community. The overall cost is drastically less expensive, especially when you calculate in the health care costs of chronic diseases from poor dietary and lifestyle choices, loss of work productivity due to illness, and the negative environmental impacts of conventional farming practices from the commercial food industry.

> **"You are going to want to give up. Don't!"**
>
> ~ Unknown

Eat well
Move daily
Hydrate often
Sleep lots
Love more
Repeat for life

Now, let's get cooking!

PART 2

LET'S GET COOKING!

IN THIS PART:

Great Beginnings

Bring on the Veggies

More For Carnivores

Dips, Snacks, and Apps

Sweetness

Beverages

For Our Furry Family Members

GREAT BEGINNINGS

Power Kave
Pumpkin Spice Latte Chia Pudding
Vanilla Pecan Chia Seed Pudding
Blueberry Vanilla Chia Seed Pudding
Banana Pancakes
Banana Muffins
Power Breakfast Bowls
Bacon, Onion, & Asparagus Frittata
Coconut Milk Yogurt
Avocado & Egg Cups
Veggie Packed Egg Cups
Power Smoothie
Green Protein Smoothie
Dark Chocolate Banana Smoothie
Ginger, Turmeric, & Mango Smoothie

breakfast

Breakfast is often viewed as the most important meal of the day, yet now, with diet trends like Intermittent Fasting, breakfast is often omitted. The great news is that these delicious recipes can be enjoyed throughout the day. Enjoy these wonderful meals whenever you are "breaking a fast"!

 **SMART INGREDIENTS**

Sea Salt: Pink Himalayan sea salt or Grey Celtic sea salt.

Canned Coconut Milk: Full fat. Check that there are no added thickeners or gums and it is in a BPA-free can. Just coconut and water.

Chocolate: 70% cocoa content. Be sure to check the label to ensure there are no added sugars.

Protein Powder: I use *Designs for Health PurePaleo* and *Orgain Organic Protein* plant-based powders.

Chocolate Chips: I use gluten, dairy, nut, and soy-free chocolate chips brand Enjoy Life.

Collagen Powder Notes: I alternate between *Vital Nutrients Marine Collagen* and *Designs for Health Whole Body Collagen*.

Bacon: nitrate-free, nitrite-free, sugar-free.

Butter: I use grass-fed *Kerry Gold*.

Frozen: Use an organic, frozen option to speed up the recipe. Check for additives, preservatives, and other unwanted ingredients before you buy.

Power Kave

I supercharge my morning coffee with healthy fats, collagen, immune-boosting mushrooms, and protein to kick start my day. Always select organic coffee beans as non-organic/conventional versions are high in pesticides. And for those of us who do not speak Hungarian, kave, means coffee.

INGREDIENTS

6-8-oz. of coffee
½-1 Tbsp. grass-fed, butter
1 scoop collagen powder
1 tsp. to 1 Tbsp. MCT oil
1 scoop mushroom powder

INSTRUCTIONS

Prepare the coffee and whisk or blend in the ingredients. I use a mini immersion blender.

MCT Oil Notes: Use C8 oil only, which is the potent oil within coconut oil that converts directly to energy; I use Designs for Health KTO-C8-100.

Mushroom Powder: some of my favorite immune-boosting mushrooms: Cordyceps, Reishi, Maitake, Lion's Mane, Chaga, Mesima, Royal Sun (Agaricus) Blazei, Shitake, Enokitake, Meshima, Tremella; Four Sigmatic has a great blend.

breakfast

Pumpkin Spice Latte Chia Pudding

INGREDIENTS

¼ cup chia seeds
1 cup coconut milk
2 Tbsp. raw maple syrup
¼ cup pumpkin puree
1 tsp. pumpkin pie spice
½ tsp. vanilla extract

Optional Toppings:
Coconut Whipped Cream
¼ tsp. cinnamon

INSTRUCTIONS

Mix all the chia pudding ingredients in a bowl with a lid for 1-2 minutes until everything is well incorporated or process in a blender. Cover or pour into large mouth mason jars and place in the fridge to firm up for at least 2 hours, or ideally overnight. Add optional toppings before serving.

Great Beginnings

Vanilla Pecan Chia Pudding

INGREDIENTS

¼ cup chia seeds
1 cup almond milk
1 tsp. vanilla extract
1 Tbsp. raw maple syrup
2 Tbsp. dried pitted dates, roughly chopped
2 Tbsp. raw pecans, roughly chopped

INSTRUCTIONS

Place all of the ingredients in a blender and blend for about 15-20 seconds. Pour into a glass bowl with a cover or large mouth mason jars and refrigerate for at least 4 hours, or ideally overnight.

breakfast

Blueberry Vanilla Chia Pudding

INGREDIENTS

6 Tbsp. chia seeds
2 cups coconut or nut milk
6-8 Tbsp. blueberries
½ tsp. vanilla extract

INSTRUCTIONS

Combine chia seeds, nut milk, blueberries, along with a dash of vanilla and an optional dab of honey in a blender. Allow to set in the fridge for 4 hours or ideally overnight. Top with fresh or frozen berries, coconut whipped cream, a dash of cinnamon, or a drizzle of raw honey or maple syrup.

- Reminder: use raw unsweetened ingredients
- Try different berries like raspberries and blueberries, fruits like mangos and bananas, and different nut or oat milk. Here are a few of my favorites:

Mango Coconut: 2 large fresh mangos (one added to a blender and one peeled and diced for the topping), ½ cup chia seeds, 2 cups coconut milk, and 2 Tbsp. maple syrup

Maple Almond: ¼ cup chia seeds, 1 cup almond milk, 2 Tbsp. almond butter, 1-2 Tbsp. maple syrup, 2 Tbsp. cocoa powder, 1 tsp. vanilla extract, and ¼ tsp. cinnamon

Coconut Banana: 1 ripe banana, ½ cup coconut milk, and 2 Tbsp. chia seeds

Great Beginnings

Banana Pancakes

INGREDIENTS

2 organic eggs
1 banana (the riper, the better)
½ Tbsp. olive oil

Optional:
½ tsp. cinnamon
2-4 Tbsp. fresh or frozen blueberries

INSTRUCTIONS

Whisk the eggs together in a medium bowl. Break the banana into chunks and use a fork to mash it into the whisked eggs. Whisk together until well blended. Add in the cinnamon and blueberries, if using. Heat the olive oil in a skillet over medium heat. Pour pancake mix onto the heated skillet and cook until edges begin to brown. Keep a close eye on the pancakes as they tend to cook quickly and may only need a few minutes. Flip and cook for about 30-60 seconds on the other side or until cooked through.

Remove to plate and top with more cinnamon, fresh blueberries, raw maple syrup and/or whipped coconut cream, as desired.

Coconut Whipped Cream-pg. 142.

Banana Muffins

INGREDIENTS

1 cup natural peanut butter
2 medium bananas
2 organic eggs
½ tsp. baking soda
1 tsp. raw apple cider vinegar
1 Tbsp. raw honey
⅛ tsp. vanilla extract

Optional:
⅛ cup mini chocolate chips

- I make a double recipe and toast them before eating throughout the week
- Great for a quick breakfast, snack, pre-workout or post-workout treat

INSTRUCTIONS

Preheat the oven to 400°F. Lightly grease a mini or standard muffin tray with avocado oil or use silicone or unbleached muffin tin liners. Place all ingredients, except the chocolate chips, into the blender and blend well. Stir in chocolate chips, if using, or sprinkle them on top. Pour batter into silicone baking cups or greased or lined muffin tin, about ⅔–¾ full (the muffins rise a lot during baking). Bake for 8-9 minutes for mini muffins or 15-18 minutes for regular muffins and check often. Be careful not to overcook! I prefer them moist and usually remove them towards the sooner end.

Place the cooled muffins in the refrigerator and enjoy within 5 days.

Peanut Butter: check ingredients to ensure there are no added sugar or oils.

Bananas: the riper the better. I often use frozen.

Great Beginnings

Power Breakfast Bowls

Power Breakfast Bowls are antioxidant-packed and anti-inflammatory. These tasty bowls are easy to make ahead of time for a quick breakfast on the go.

INGREDIENTS

1 cup cooked quinoa
¼ cup steel-cut gluten-free, oats
1 can coconut milk
¼ tsp. cinnamon
2 Tbsp. raw maple syrup
3 Tbsp. raw seeds-chia, flax, hemp, or combination
Raw nuts, berries, and seeds

INSTRUCTIONS

Cook quinoa as per instructions on the package using only water (and not with chicken, vegetable, or bone broth). Mix 1 cup cooked quinoa with steel-cut oats, ½ can coconut milk, cinnamon, maple syrup and chia, flax and/or hemp seeds. Allow to soak for at least 2 hours, or ideally overnight. Spoon out the desired portion and top with remaining coconut milk, nuts, seeds, and berries.

- Fill 1 cup sized Pyrex dishes halfway with the quinoa mix, pour on a little coconut milk, and add the berries for a quick weekday morning breakfast or breakfast on the go.
- Double the recipe to make 8 servings!

Seeds: I often use 2-3 Tbsp. of each type of seeds.

My Favorite Nuts, Seeds & Berries: chopped walnuts, pecans, blueberries, raspberries, blackberries, strawberries, hemp, and flax seeds.

breakfast

Bacon, Onion, & Asparagus Frittata

*Breakfast frittatas are an easy on-the-go way to start your day!
This recipe provides you the flexibility to utilize the freshest local ingredients you can find.
It is also an easy and delicious way to increase your daily vegetable intake.*

INGREDIENTS

½-1 Tbsp. avocado oil
4 slices of bacon
1 small onion
1 bunch of asparagus, roughly chopped
8 organic eggs
½ tsp. sea salt
½ tsp. black pepper
½ tsp. paprika
1 avocado, diced

INSTRUCTIONS

Preheat the oven to 350°F. Cook bacon over medium-high heat until lightly browned, about 2-3 minutes. Add onion and asparagus (or any other vegetables and fresh herbs you desire), and sauté for 2-3 minutes or until onions are translucent. Whisk the eggs together and add the bacon and vegetable mixture, sea salt, and pepper to the eggs. Pour into a prepared pie dish lightly oiled with avocado oil. Bake for 25-35 minutes, depending on your oven, until the edges are browned, and the frittata is cooked thoroughly. Remove from the oven, sprinkle with paprika and allow to cool for about 10 minutes before slicing. Serve with avocado on top and add some fresh chopped herbs like parsley or cilantro if desired.

My Favorite Veggies and Herbs: To mix it up, try a combination of seasonal vegetables and fresh herbs: zucchini, mushrooms, spinach, summer squash, garlic, basil, chives, green onions, dill, and tomatoes.

Great Beginnings

Coconut Milk Yogurt

INGREDIENTS

1 can coconut milk
2 probiotic capsules

Fun Fact: The food industry adds unhealthy thickeners to commercially produced yogurt to prevent separation because consumers do not like it. Either stir it in or put the yogurt in the refrigerator and then scoop off the creamy top layer.

INSTRUCTIONS

Empty the can of coconut milk into a clean glass jar or bowl (I often use a wide mouth mason jar). Add the capsules of probiotics and stir. Cover the bowl with a cheesecloth or a paper towel and secure it with a rubber band (or if you use a wide mouth mason jar, use just the ring portion of the top). Place in a warm place, like inside the oven with the light on, but do not turn on the oven! Allow to sit undisturbed for at least 24–48 hours.

Once your yogurt has activated (for the above stated 24-48 hours) refrigerate for at least 2 hours to thicken and cool.

- It's natural for the yogurt to separate.
- Top with fresh berries, hemp seeds, and a drizzle of raw maple syrup.
- Always use "organic full-fat" coconut milk; ingredients only should contain "coconut and water."

breakfast

Avocado & Egg Cups

Egg cups are a perfect quick weekday meal.

INGREDIENTS

1 medium avocado
2 organic eggs
1 slice of bacon, cooked and crumbled
Pinch of sea salt

INSTRUCTIONS

Preheat the oven to 425°F. Cut the avocado in half and remove the seed. With a spoon, scoop out some of the avocado, so there is room for the egg. Place avocado halves in a muffin pan to keep the avocado stable while cooking. Crack each egg and add them to the inside of your avocado halves. Sprinkle with a pinch of sea salt and top with crumbled cooked bacon.

Cook for 14-16 minutes until the whites are cooked thoroughly, and the yolk is cooked to your desired level. Serve warm.

Great Beginnings

Veggie Packed Egg Cups

Egg cups are a perfect quick weekday meal.
They reheat quickly in the toaster oven or microwave.

INGREDIENTS

2 pieces of bacon (optional)
12 organic eggs
1 Tbsp. olive oil
1 cup fresh vegetables, chopped and sautéed
Sea salt and pepper
1 Tbsp. of chopped fresh herbs

INSTRUCTIONS

Preheat the oven to 400°F. Cook bacon for 6-8 minutes and allow bacon to cool on a paper towel. While the bacon is cooling, sauté the vegetables in the rendered bacon grease or olive oil. Spray the muffin tin with avocado oil. Break the bacon into crumbles. Crack the eggs into a bowl and whip them. Add in the bacon crumbles, sautéed vegetables, and sprinkle with fresh herbs, sea salt, and pepper. Pour the mixture into each muffin tin about halfway. Cook for 12-15 minutes.

My Favorite Veggies: onions, peppers, and zucchini.

My Favorite Herbs: garlic, rosemary, and parsley, or dried garlic powder and dried parsley. Dried rosemary is very tough and does not soften in this recipe; therefore, if you are going to use rosemary, only use fresh.

breakfast

SMOOTHIES

To quickly increase nutrient intake use greens, protein, or fiber powders. "Smoothies" are great because they can be as simple or complex as you desire. Try experimenting with the ingredients you have on hand and try new combinations. Purchase ripe, in-season, and ingredients for the highest nutrient content and the lowest amount of pesticide residuals.

Power Smoothie

INGREDIENTS

2 large handfuls fresh or frozen spinach
1 cup frozen berries
½ of an avocado
1 Tbsp. ground flax seeds
1 Tbsp. coconut oil
½ tsp. cinnamon
1 cup non-dairy milk

INSTRUCTIONS

Place spinach leaves in a blender with half the non-dairy milk and blend for a few seconds. Add all the other ingredients and blend until smooth.

My Favorite Fruit: pineapple, blueberries, and cherries. Other berries or berry blends with raspberries and blackberries have a lot of seeds that may get caught in your teeth.

Milk Options: coconut, hemp, or almond milk.

Great Beginnings

Green Protein Smoothie

INGREDIENTS

1 banana
2 dried dates, pitted
2 cups fresh or frozen spinach
2 Tbsp. almond butter
1 Tbsp. chia seeds
2 Tbsp. hemp seeds
1 cup non-dairy milk

INSTRUCTIONS

Place spinach leaves in a blender with half the non-dairy milk and blend for a few seconds. Add all the other ingredients and blend until smooth. Enjoy immediately.

Milk Options: coconut, hemp, or almond milk.

breakfast

Dark Chocolate Banana Smoothie

INGREDIENTS

1 cup fresh or frozen spinach
1 banana
1 cup almond milk
3 Tbsp. chia seeds
2 Tbsp. cocoa powder
½ tsp. vanilla extract

INSTRUCTIONS

Add all the ingredients and blend until smooth. Enjoy immediately.

Milk Options: you can substitute hemp or coconut milk.

Ginger, Turmeric, & Mango Smoothie

INGREDIENTS

½ cup frozen mango
½ banana
1 cup coconut milk
½ Tbsp. ground ginger
½ Tbsp. ground turmeric
½ Tbsp. cinnamon
1 Tbsp. raw honey
1 Tbsp. chia seeds
¼ tsp. black pepper

INSTRUCTIONS

Add all the ingredients and blend until smooth. Enjoy immediately.

Milk Options: you can substitute hemp or almond milk.

Great Beginnings

BRING ON THE VEGGIES

Buddah Bowls
Tahini Sauce
Quinoa with Pecans, Raisins, & Apricots
Vegetable Curry
Curried Sweet Potato & Apple Soup
Sweet Potato & Cauliflower Taco Bowls
Collard Green Wraps
Collard Greens
Cauliflower Mash
Coconut Lime Cauliflower Rice
Pesto
Roasted Pea Soup with Pumpkin & Hemp Seeds
Sauerkraut
Veggie Sheet Pan Deliciousness
Natural Salad Dressings
Mediterranean Salad
Crunchy Salad
Quinoa Salad
Wilted Kale Salad

veg out

SMART INGREDIENTS

Sea Salt: Pink Himalayan sea salt or Grey Celtic sea salt

Canned Coconut Milk: Full fat. Check that there are no added thickeners or gums and it is in a BPA-free can.

Frozen: Use an organic, frozen option to speed up the recipe. Check for additives, preservatives, and other unwanted ingredients before you buy.

Butter: I use *Kerry Gold*.

Buddha Bowls

Buddha bowls are another great meal with a million different variations possible. The recipe here is to help guide you, but remember to experiment with ingredients you have on hand and also try new ingredients, focusing on ripe, in-season, and organic produce.

INGREDIENTS

2 cups of cooked quinoa
Roasted vegetables (see notes below)
Nutritional yeast (the amount depends on which vegetables you use)
Sea salt
Baby spinach or baby power greens mix
Tahini sauce (optional)
Organic sprouts

INSTRUCTIONS

Cook quinoa as per package instructions using bone broth recipe on page 106. Chop vegetables into bite-size pieces and coat with avocado oil. Roast at 400°F until vegetables are crispy on edges. Sprinkle nutritional yeast on cauliflower. Sprinkle sea salt on roasted vegetables. Arrange quinoa and greens in a bowl and top with roasted vegetables. Drizzle with tahini sauce and garnish with sprouts.

- Leftovers are fabulous cold for lunches or reheat quickly for weeknight dinner.
- Add some extra plant-based protein with chickpeas or tofu.

Roasted Vegetables: try any combination of sweet potatoes, cauliflower, broccoli, asparagus, carrots, brussels sprouts, zucchini, onion, or garlic. Sweet potatoes usually take around 45 minutes total, carrots, cauliflower, and broccoli take about 25 minutes, then asparagus, zucchini, onions, and garlic are usually done in about 15 minutes.

veggies

Tahini Sauce

The perfect topper for Buddha Bowls!

INGREDIENTS

¼ cup tahini
3 Tbsp. lemon juice
2 cloves of garlic
1 tsp. coconut aminos
1 Tbsp. raw maple syrup
1 Tbsp. sriracha or other hot sauce, to taste

INSTRUCTIONS

Blend all ingredients in a small food processor, mixer, or blender. Taste and add more ingredients as desired. Keep in an airtight container in the refrigerator for up to one week.

Quinoa with Pecans, Raisins, & Apricots

INGREDIENTS

3 Tbsp. pecans, chopped
1 cup quinoa
⅓ cup dried apricots, chopped
¼ cup raisins
2 scallions, finely chopped
1 Tbsp. fresh cilantro, chopped
1 Tbsp. lemon juice
1 Tbsp. olive oil
½ tsp. sea salt

INSTRUCTIONS

Cook quinoa in water per package instructions and allow to cool to room temperature. Toast the pecans in a skillet over medium heat for 3-4 minutes. Move to a plate to cool. In a large bowl, mix the cooked quinoa, apricots, raisins, scallion, cilantro, and toasted pecans. Stir in lemon juice, olive oil, and sea salt; mix well. Best served at room temperature.

Vegetable Curry

This curry freezes well, which is great for quick weeknight dinners or meal prep lunches.

INGREDIENTS

2-3 Tbsp. avocado oil
1 sweet potato, peeled and chopped
2-3 cups broccoli florets, fresh or frozen, chopped into bite-sized pieces
1 onion, diced
3-4 cloves of garlic, diced
1 Tbsp. ginger root, freshly grated
1 can (13.5oz) of coconut milk + 1 can of water
3 Tbsp. curry powder
2 tsp. cumin
1 Tbsp. raw maple syrup
2-3 cups fresh spinach leaves
1 cup jasmine rice or brown rice ramen, cooked

Optional:
1 tsp. cayenne
Organic curry leaves

INSTRUCTIONS

Cook rice according to the package (using bone broth is best). Heat oil in a large cast-iron or "sauté" pan. Cook onion until softened, about 1-2 minutes, and then add garlic and ginger. Stir and cook for another minute. Add in curry powder, cumin, and cayenne, if using. Stir until well mixed. Add sweet potatoes, broccoli, and any other vegetables you want to add, but do not add the spinach here. Pour in coconut milk and then fill the can with water; add water to cover the vegetables, stir in maple syrup, top with curry leaves, if using. Simmer for 10-15 minutes or until vegetables are cooked. Remove from heat and stir in baby spinach leaves until wilted.

My Favorite Protein Add-ins: chicken, chickpeas, or tofu

My Favorite Veggies: broccoli and sweet potatoes

Curried Sweet Potato & Apple Soup

INGREDIENTS

1 Tbsp. olive oil + an additional 2 tsp. for finishing topping
1 onion, chopped
3 cloves of garlic, chopped
1 tsp. fresh ginger root, finely chopped
1 tsp. curry powder
½ tsp. ground cumin
½ tsp. sea salt
¼ tsp. cinnamon powder
A handful of curry leaves (optional)
2 cups of water
2-3 medium sweet potatoes, peeled and cut into chunks
2 medium apples, peeled, cored, and cut into chunks

INSTRUCTIONS

Heat olive oil in a Dutch oven or large saucepan over medium heat. Add onion, stir and cook until tender, about 5 minutes. Add garlic, ginger, curry powder, cumin, sea salt, and cinnamon. Stir constantly for about 1 minute. Add curry leaves (optional), water, sweet potatoes, apples, and bring to a boil over high heat. Reduce heat to simmer, stirring often, and cook for about 20 minutes or until the sweet potatoes are very tender. Remove curry leaves, if used. Use an immersion blender or puree soup in batches in a food processor or blender until very smooth.

Serve warm topped with herbs and a drizzle of olive oil.

Topping: ¼ cup fresh parsley or cilantro, chopped

Sweet Potato & Cauliflower Taco Bowls

This recipe has several steps, but well worth the effort.

INGREDIENTS

1 head cauliflower, cut into bite-sized florets
1 large sweet potato, diced into ½-inch cubes
1 Tbsp. avocado oil
1 tsp. chili powder
1 tsp. ground cumin
1 tsp. smoked paprika
½ tsp. garlic powder
½ tsp. dried oregano
½ tsp. sea salt
1 lime, juiced or 1 Tbsp. lime juice
1 (14-oz.) can black beans, drained and rinsed

INSTRUCTIONS

Preheat the oven to 425°F. Line a large baking sheet with parchment paper and set aside. Place the cauliflower florets and diced sweet potato in a large bowl. Drizzle the avocado oil over top and sprinkle the chili powder, cumin, paprika, garlic powder, oregano, and salt. Squeeze the lime juice over top and stir well. Transfer the veggies to the prepared baking dish, arranging everything in a single layer, with lots of space. Roast the veggies for 25 minutes, giving the baking sheets a good stir about halfway through. Add the black beans to the sheet pan, seasoning with another pinch of salt, then place the pan back in the oven for 5 more minutes to heat the black beans through. Remove from the oven and set aside.

Serve with Cashew Lime Crema, Avocado Mash and Garnish (see next page)

Assemble:
Use a base of quinoa, Coconut Lime Cauliflower Rice- pg. 87 and top with a generous scoop of roasted veggies. Drizzle Cashew Lime Crema and Avocado Mash on top. Sprinkle freshly chopped cilantro, diced jalapeño, and a squeeze of lime.

Cashew Lime Crema

Great addition to Sweet Potato & Cauliflower taco bowl along with Avocado Mash.

INGREDIENTS

¼ cup raw unsalted cashews
1 jalapeño pepper
1 clove garlic
½ tsp. chili powder
½ tsp. smoked paprika
½ ground cumin
¼ tsp. sea salt
½ cup of water
1 lime, juiced or 1 Tbsp. lime juice

INSTRUCTIONS

Add cashews, jalapeño, garlic clove, water, lime juice, chili powder, paprika, cumin, and salt to a high-speed blender. Blend to combine.

Transfer to a bowl and set aside or store in an airtight container in the refrigerator for up to one week.

Garnish: chopped fresh cilantro, lime wedges, and diced jalapeños

---

Avocado Mash:
1 medium ripe avocado
1 lime, juiced
½ tsp. sea salt

Mash all together with a fork in a bowl to your desired consistency.

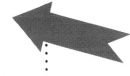

Bring on the Veggies

Collard Green Wraps

*Great for a quick lunch, make-ahead to meal prep,
or cut smaller for an appetizer.*

INGREDIENTS

1 large collard green leaf
1 Tbsp. hummus
¼ avocado, sliced
1-2 radishes, sliced thin
1 small carrot, sliced thin or shredded
¼ cucumber, sliced thin
6-8 baby tomatoes, sliced lengthwise
¼ pepper, sliced thin
¼ cup sprouts

INSTRUCTIONS

Remove center rib from collard leaves by cutting them in half long way. Slice or shred vegetables. Place a small dollop of hummus on each collard green half and smooth along the center. Add a few slices or shreds of each vegetable and top with sprouts. If making appetizers, cut into small pinwheels and place a toothpick in them.

Optional Add-Ins:
- Guacamole; recipe included-pg. 136
- Spicy Black Bean Dip-pg. 132
- Spicy avocado hummus-pg. 135
- Get creative with other veggies, fresh herbs, sliced meats, or cheeses.

Collard Greens Prep: Wash and remove center rib. Then, cut lengthwise. 1 large leaf = 2 wraps

veggies

Instapot Collard Greens

Simple, quick, easy, delicious, and nutritious.

INGREDIENTS

2 bunches of collard greens
8-12 cloves of garlic, smashed
¼ cup of water
2 Tbsp. avocado or olive oil
½ tsp. paprika

Optional:
1-2 pork or beef bones
½ tsp. cayenne pepper

1-2 Tbsp. raw apple cider vinegar (add just before serving)

INSTRUCTIONS

Place the Instapot on "sauté." Add oil and garlic. Cook for 2-3 minutes, but do not allow the garlic to burn. Add the water and dried spices. Turn off the Instapot. Add the collard greens, bones, if using, and select 5 minutes "manual" high pressure. Once cooked, allow steam to naturally release for 10-15 minutes. (Use caution when opening as the steam is very hot). Scoop out desired amount and drizzle with apple cider vinegar.

- This recipe can be made on the stovetop in a saucepan over medium-low heat for 30-45 minutes. Be sure to wait until the final 5-10 minutes of cooking time to add in the garlic for maximum medicinal potency.
- Instapot/Pressure cooker breaks down the fibrous collard green leaves better.

Collard Greens: 2 bunches = about 2 lbs. Wash and remove center rib. Then, cut or tear into approximately 2-inch x 4-inch pieces.

Cayenne Pepper: The heat is great for digestion.

Cauliflower Mash

INGREDIENTS

1 medium head of cauliflower or 1 (12-oz.) bag of frozen cauliflower florets
2 cloves of garlic
1 Tbsp. grass-fed butter
½ tsp. sea salt
½ tsp. black pepper
½ tsp. granulated garlic

Green onion for garnish

INSTRUCTIONS

Cut cauliflower into small chunks, if using fresh. Place cauliflower florets, cloves of garlic, and a dash of sea salt in a medium saucepan and cover with water. Cover and bring the pot to a boil. Reduce heat and simmer for about 10 minutes or until the florets are fork tender and drain. Place florets, butter, sea salt, pepper, and granulated garlic in a food processor (you can also use an immersion blender or stand up blender) and process until smooth. Add more granulated garlic, sea salt, and pepper to taste. Serve hot, topped with chopped green onions.

- Serve with Veggie-Packed Meatloaf-pg. 113

Topping: 2-3 fresh green onions, chopped

Coconut Lime Cauliflower Rice

INGREDIENTS

1 Tbsp. avocado oil
2 green onions, sliced thin
2 cloves of garlic, minced
1 (12-oz.) bag of frozen riced cauliflower
3+ Tbsp. full-fat coconut milk (with no added thickeners or gums and it is in a BPA-free can)
Juice 1 lime or use 1 Tbsp. lime juice
¼-½ cup fresh cilantro, chopped
Sea salt

INSTRUCTIONS

Heat oil in "sauté" pan over medium heat. Add green onions and "sauté" for a minute or 2, until soft. Add garlic and cook for about 30 seconds. Pour in cauliflower rice and 3 Tbsp. of coconut milk. Cook for about 3 minutes on medium heat, stirring frequently, add in more coconut milk if needed, 1 tsp. at a time. Ideally, the cauliflower should be al dente and not soft. Turn off the heat and stir in lime juice, fresh cilantro, sea salt, and pepper. Add more lime juice or sea salt to taste.

- Serve with Spicy Squash-pg. 95 and Spicy Black Bean Dip-pg. 132 in the Carnitas Bowls-pg. 109

Pesto

INGREDIENTS

1 Tbsp. lemon juice
¼ cup pine nuts or pecans, toasted
¼ cup shelled, raw, hemp seeds/hearts
½ cup hemp seed, avocado, or olive oil (+ 2 Tbsp. for preservation)
1-2 cloves of garlic, chopped
¼ tsp. sea salt
2 cups fresh basil leaves

INSTRUCTIONS

Toast the pine nuts or pecans in a small fry pan for a few minutes over medium heat; be cautious not to burn them. Mix all ingredients except the lemon juice and oil in a food processor or blender. Once dry ingredients are well blended, add in the lemon juice and oil. Serve with gluten-free pasta, spaghetti squash, or raw zoodles.

- I often use the flowers and tops of my basil plants.
- If you are not using the pesto immediately, pour a few Tbsp. of oil on top of the pesto to help preserve the basil.
- This pesto freezes well as long as you put a few Tbsp. of oil on the top to help preserve the basil.

Roasted Pea Soup with Pumpkin & Hemp Seeds

INGREDIENTS

1 cup fresh or frozen peas, shelled
2 Tbsp. olive oil, divided
1 leek, white & light green parts, thinly sliced
3 cloves of garlic, chopped
1 Tbsp. fresh or dried rosemary, chopped
½ tsp. fresh or dried thyme leaves
¼ cup dry white wine
2 cups stock/broth
⅛ cup pumpkin and hemp seeds
2 sprigs of fresh parsley, chopped (stems & leaves)
Sea salt & pepper

INSTRUCTIONS

Preheat the oven to 400°F. If using fresh peas, add to a pot of salted boiling water and cook for about 3 to 5 minutes until tender and then drain. Toss peas with 1 Tbsp. olive oil, season with sea salt and pepper, and spread in a single layer over a large baking sheet. Roast for about 15 minutes, until lightly browned.

Heat the remaining 1 Tbsp. olive oil in a large pot over medium heat. Once hot, add the leeks and cook, occasionally stirring until softened, about 6 minutes. Add the garlic, rosemary, and thyme; season with sea salt and pepper and cook 2 minutes more. Add in the wine and stock or broth and bring to a boil. Lower the heat to a simmer, stir in the peas, and cook for about 2 minutes. Use a blender or food processor to purée the soup. Serve warm, topped with the seeds and parsley.

Stock/Broth: vegetable, chicken or Bone Broth recipe-pg. 106

Sauerkraut

INGREDIENTS

1 large head of cabbage, shredded (retain outer leaves)
1 Tbsp. sea salt per head of cabbage; and 1¼ tsp. sea salt for brine
1 cup water

- I use a small glass cup on top of the cabbage leaves to ensure they stay submerged. Place the jars in a shallow dish as the liquid may leak out during fermentation, which is completely normal.
- Check on the jars daily to ensure the cabbage is submerged and release excess gas build-up. If the liquid is below the cabbage, fill with more brine solution as per the ratio in the recipe. Let it ferment long enough to allow all of the fermentation stages to happen. This depends on several factors, including the size of the jars used and the temperature of the room.
- You can tell if a ferment is safe to eat if it smells sour and pleasant. If it smells rancid, like broccoli or lettuce rotting in your fridge, or has any discoloration, then it should be thrown out.

INSTRUCTIONS

Shred the cabbage, saving several outer leaves for packing. Place the shredded cabbage in a large bowl. I use my food processor, but you can chop it by hand. Add 1 Tbsp. sea salt, massage the cabbage to release the juices, and mix it up. I often make several batches at once, shredding several heads of cabbage at a time. Increase the sea salt to approximately 1 Tbsp. per head of cabbage shredded. This will vary depending on several factors, including the size of the head of cabbage, the grind, and the saltiness of your sea salt. Allow it to sit for 10-15 minutes.

Mix the remaining 1 ¼ tsp. sea salt with the 1 cup of water. Taste the liquid at the bottom of the cabbage bowl and the saltwater; they should be the same level of saltiness. If not salty enough, add ½ tsp sea salt and massage the cabbage and taste the water again. Repeat until the saltiness is the same. If the cabbage is too salty, add 1-2 Tbsp. water to the cabbage and mix it up. Repeat until it's not too salty. Put into large mason jars or glass jars filled to about 2-3 inches from the top. Place two outer leaves on top to ensure the cabbage stays submerged in the liquid and place the top on the jar(s).

veggies

Roasted Brussels Sprouts
sheet pan deliciousness

INGREDIENTS

1 lb. Brussels sprouts (trim ends and cut in half)
5-7 cloves of garlic, roughly chopped (ideal to have big chunks that will not burn)
1-2 Tbsp. avocado oil
½ tsp. sea salt

INSTRUCTIONS

Preheat the oven to 400°F. Toss Brussels and garlic in the oil. Place Brussels cut side down on a rimmed sheet pan lined with parchment paper. Sprinkle it with sea salt and pepper. Cook at 400°F for 20-30 minutes, depending on oven type and desired crispiness.

sheet pan deliciousness

Roasted Carrots

INGREDIENTS

2 lbs. carrots, sliced diagonal and of uniform thickness (about ½-inch thick)
2 Tbsp. avocado oil
½ tsp. sea salt
¼ tsp. black pepper
½ tsp. cumin powder
½ tsp. turmeric powder
½ tsp. ginger powder

Garnish with chopped, fresh parsley

INSTRUCTIONS

Preheat the oven to 425°F. Cut carrots diagonal in uniform size to ensure equal cooking. Lay a piece of parchment paper on a large rimmed sheet pan. Toss carrots in avocado oil and sprinkle with dried herbs, sea salt, and pepper. Spread out the carrots on the sheet pan and ensure none are touching to ensure proper cooking. Cook for 10 minutes and then flip and cook for another 8-10 minutes depending on desired doneness and oven temperatures. When cooked, remove from the oven and sprinkle with fresh parsley.

Black Pepper: necessary to activate the bioavailability and absorption of the turmeric

veggies

Cabbage Steaks
sheet pan deliciousness

Great for meatless meals or as a delicious side! This is best served freshly cooked. I often cook one large steak or two small steaks per person as a side dish.

INGREDIENTS

Cabbage, cut into 1-inch slices
1-1½ Tbsp. avocado oil
2-3 cloves of garlic, smashed
Sea salt
Black pepper

INSTRUCTIONS

Preheat the oven to 400°F and line a rimmed baking sheet with parchment paper. Place cabbage steaks on the baking sheet. Rub with smashed garlic or sprinkle with garlic granules. Drizzle oil over the cabbage steaks. Sprinkle sea salt and pepper on the steaks. Roast for 30 minutes and then flip. Roast for another 30 minutes until the edges are crispy and browned.

Avocado Oil: add more depending on how many 'steaks' you make.

Garlic: opt for 2-3 tsp. garlic granules; again, adjust the amount depending on how many steaks you are making.

Bring on the Veggies

sheet pan deliciousness

Butternut Squash

This is one of my husband's favorite dishes! It is simple to cook, nutritious, delicious to eat, and reheats well to use for several side dishes.

INGREDIENTS

1 medium to large butternut squash
3-4 Tbsp. olive oil
Sea salt and black pepper
¼ cup of water

INSTRUCTIONS

Preheat the oven to 375°F. Cut butternut squash in half lengthwise, scoop out, and discard the seeds (or clean to use to grow your own or place in the compost bin). Place both squash halves, cut side up, in a rimmed sheet pan lined with parchment paper. Drizzle with olive oil and sprinkle with sea salt and pepper. Turn the squash cut side down and pour the water into the pan. Pierce the skin several times with a fork. Bake in the oven, uncovered, for about 45 minutes or until the squash is softened. Be sure to check occasionally to ensure the squash is not burning. Remove when cooked and allow to cool for about 10 minutes. Scoop out the flesh with a spoon.

veggies

sheet pan deliciousness

Spicy Squash

Excellent addition to Carnitas-pg. 109 and Buddha Bowls-pg. 78

INGREDIENTS

3-4 medium zucchini, summer squash, or a combination
2 Tbsp. avocado oil
½ tsp. chili powder
½ granulated garlic
¼ tsp. cayenne powder
Pinch of sea salt and black pepper
Juice 1 lime or use 1 Tbsp. lime juice
2 Tbsp. fresh cilantro, chopped

INSTRUCTIONS

Preheat the oven to 425°F and place parchment paper on a rimmed baking sheet. Mix diced squash, avocado oil, dried herbs, sea salt, and pepper in a medium bowl until well mixed. Spread evenly on the baking sheet and roast for 20-25 minutes, or until browned. Sprinkle with lime juice and fresh cilantro.

sheet pan deliciousness

Spaghetti Squash

INGREDIENTS

1 spaghetti squash
2 Tbsp. avocado oil
Pinch of sea salt and black pepper

INSTRUCTIONS

Preheat the oven to 400°F. Cut the squash in half lengthwise, and use caution as they are challenging to cut. Remove the seeds with a spoon. Pierce the skin several times with a fork on all sides. Drizzle the inside of the cut squash with avocado oil and sprinkle with sea salt and pepper. Place the two halves cut side down on a rimmed sheet pan covered in parchment paper and cook for at least 45 minutes. Check the squash occasionally, and it is ready when you can easily stick a fork in it. Allow it to cool for at least 10 minutes and then use a fork to gently scrape out the flesh into strands.

- Serve with Organic Pesto-pg. 88 or Bolognese Sauce-pg. 112
- Also delicious served plain, drizzled with olive oil and sprinkled with sea salt.

veggies

sheet pan deliciousness

Maple Carrots & Beets

INGREDIENTS

5 large carrots peeled and sliced
4 medium beets peeled and diced
2 Tbsp. avocado oil
Sea salt and black pepper to taste
2 Tbsp. grass-fed butter
3 Tbsp. raw maple syrup
2-3 Tbsp. chopped fresh parsley

INSTRUCTIONS

Preheat the oven to 425°F and move the rack to the middle position. Cut the beets and carrots into pieces that are roughly the same size and place the pieces on a large rimmed sheet pan. Drizzle the olive oil onto the beets and carrots and add sea salt and pepper. Toss until they're coated. Spread them out in an even layer. Roast for about 15 minutes, or until the veggies are tender-crisp (this will vary depending on how big the pieces are and personal preference.) Take the baking sheet out of the oven and add the butter and maple syrup directly to the baking sheet. Let the butter melt, then toss it again until everything is coated. Return the baking sheet back into the oven for another 5 minutes. Top with chopped fresh parsley and serve immediately.

Roasted Carrots with Quinoa & Chickpeas

sheet pan deliciousness

INGREDIENTS

6 large or 9 medium carrots, thickly sliced
1 small onion, chopped
1 can chickpeas, drained and rinsed
2 Tbsp. olive oil
½ tsp. sea salt
¼ tsp. black pepper
1 Tbsp. fresh rosemary, chopped
3 cloves of garlic, minced
¼ cup dry white wine
1 Tbsp. lemon juice
2 cups of cooked quinoa
¼ cup pumpkin seeds
¼ cup hemp seeds
4 sprigs of fresh parsley, stems and leaves, chopped

INSTRUCTIONS

Cook quinoa per package instructions.
Preheat the oven to 375°F. In a roasting pan, combine the sliced carrots, chopped onion, chickpeas, and olive oil. Pour the white wine and lemon juice into the pan and cover with tin foil. Roast for 30 minutes, then remove the foil, add fresh rosemary and garlic, and cook for an additional 5 to 10 minutes until carrots are tender. Remove carrots from the oven and toss with quinoa, pumpkin, and hemp seeds and top with fresh parsley. Best served warm.

SALADS

Get creative! Explore new ingredients. Perfect for weekday lunches on the go. I recommend putting the salad dressing in an upcycled glass jar or bottle with a tight fitting lid.

Salad Dressing Caution:
Do not use any salad dressing that contains vegetable oil, soy oil, canola oil, or any words that you cannot pronounce. Conventional salad dressings also contain added sugar. Save time, money, and reduce your health risks by making your own at home!

Natural Salad Dressing

INGREDIENTS

½ cup olive oil or avocado oil
½ cup raw apple cider vinegar
2 Tbsp. raw pure maple syrup or raw unfiltered honey
¼ cup fresh chopped herbs

INSTRUCTIONS

Add all ingredients to a glass jar with a lid and shake well. Store in the refrigerator and allow it to warm a bit at room temperature before using. Shake well before serving.

- Use a clean glass bottle or mason jar to store salad dressing. A wide mouth option is helpful.

My Favorite Herbs: Cilantro, parsley, and rosemary; diced cloves of garlic and grated fresh ginger root

Mediterranean Salad

INGREDIENTS

1 small purple onion, finely diced
3 cups of quinoa
½ cup kalamata olives, finely diced
1 cup artichoke hearts, packed in olive oil, chopped
½ cup goat or sheep milk feta cheese, crumbled
¾ cup sun-dried tomatoes, chopped
¼ cup lemon juice
½ cup olive oil

INSTRUCTIONS

Prepare the quinoa with water according to package directions. Mix all the ingredients together and serve.

- I use quinoa made with water only for this recipe.

Crunchy Salad

INGREDIENTS

2 cups cauliflower, chopped
2 cups broccoli, chopped
1 cup purple cabbage, chopped
1 cup carrots, chopped
1½ cups fresh parsley, stems & leaves, chopped
2 celery stalks, diced
½ cup raw unsalted sunflower, hemp hearts/seeds and/or pumpkin seeds
⅓ cup dried raisins, chopped

INSTRUCTIONS

Roughly chop all the vegetables or use a food processor. Place all the vinaigrette ingredients in a bowl and whisk together. Mix the remaining salad ingredients and chopped vegetables and parsley with the vinaigrette in a large bowl and mix well. Refrigerate for at least an hour before serving. Best enjoyed within 3 days.

Vinaigrette:
3 Tbsp. olive oil
½ cup lemon juice
1 Tbsp. fresh ginger, peeled and grated
2 Tbsp. raw honey
½ tsp. sea salt

Quinoa Salad

My version of a gluten-free cold "pasta" salad and my favorite way to eat leftover quinoa.

INGREDIENTS

2 cups quinoa
½ bunch of parsley, with stems, finely chopped
1 Tbsp. lemon juice
3 Tbsp. olive oil
1-2 tsp. sea salt
A few dashes of cayenne

INSTRUCTIONS

Prepare quinoa with water according to package directions, then cool.
Mix lemon juice, olive oil, sea salt, and cayenne together. Add in the finely chopped parsley and stir in quinoa. Best served at room temperature.

veggies

Wilted Kale Salad

INGREDIENTS

1 bunch of kale, center rib removed and torn into small pieces
¼ cup olive oil
1-2 Tbsp. lemon juice
2-3 tsp. sea salt

INSTRUCTIONS

Remove the center rib from the kale leaves and break into small pieces. Place into a large bowl. Drizzle in oil, sea salt, and lemon juice. Massage vigorously by hand for 3-4 minutes.

The goal is to have about half the size from when you start. Taste and add in additional oil, sea salt, and/or lemon juice as desired. Enjoy within 3-4 days, keep in the refrigerator, and serve chilled.

Bring on the Veggies

MORE FOR THE CARNIVORE

Bone Broth
Bacon
Shrimp & Veggie Brown Rice Ramen
Carnitas
Chuck Roast
Slow Cooker Salsa Chicken
Bolognese Sauce
Veggie Packed Meatloaf
Sausage, Cabbage, & Sweet Potatoes
Chicken Curry Soup
Chicken Zoodle Soup
Beef Stew
Beef & Cabbage Soup
Beef & Broccoli Stir Fry
Sausage, Brussels Sprouts, Sweet Potato, & Apples
Sweet Italian Sausage & Veggies
Chicken Sausage, Potatoes, & Broccoli
Oven-Baked Boneless Chicken Thighs
Indian Spiced Baked Chicken
Oven-Baked Chicken Drumsticks
Dijon Salmon
Low-Cook Salmon
Shrimp Stir Fry

For meat eaters, select the highest quality meat available but consume smaller portions. There are several fabulous grass-fed beef, organic pork, organic chicken, free-range egg, and wild-caught fish merchants.

Online delivery companies include *Five Mary's, Butcher's Box, and Moink*. *Whole Foods* and *Costco* have the best selection I have found. I recently learned about and utilized a fabulous local grass-fed beef, organic chicken, free-range egg, and raw dairy merchant that delivers to my home area called *Red Tractor*. *Weston A Price Foundation* is a good resource to aid you in locating local farmers and humane butchers as they have health ambassadors throughout the country.

 **SMART INGREDIENTS**

Sea Salt: Pink Himalayan sea salt or Grey Celtic sea salt

Canned Coconut Milk: Full fat. Check that there are no added thickeners or gums and it is in a BPA-free can.

Bacon: nitrate-free, nitrite-free, and sugar-free; organic pork

Beef: Grass-fed

Pork, Chicken & Eggs: Organic

Seafood: Wild-caught

Frozen: Use an organic option to speed up the recipe. Check for additives, preservatives, and other unwanted ingredients before you buy.

Bone Broth

Use grass-fed oxtail and beef bones, and organic chicken and pork bones. Include all the collagen joints and healthy fat for this recipe. Including fat and skin are optional, but add great flavor and health benefits. The number of bones you can use will depend on the size of your Stockpot, Crock-pot, or Instapot as the bones need to be covered by water.

INGREDIENTS

Bones
Water, enough to cover the bones in whichever cooking vessel is utilized
2-4 Tbsp. raw apple cider vinegar
2-4 tsp. sea salt

INSTRUCTIONS

Roast bones on a baking sheet lined with parchment paper at 450°F for 10 minutes or until starting to brown. Place in the Crock-pot, Instapot, or Stockpot. This recipe will cook for 6 hours in an Instapot or simmer for 12 hours in a Crock-pot or Stockpot over medium-low heat. Add 2-4 Tbsp. raw apple cider vinegar, do not skip this step, as vinegar is critical to releasing the minerals from the bones. Fill the pot with enough water to cover the bones (if using an Instapot or Crock-pot, stay below the maximum fill line), leave enough room for the water to boil and steam to escape, and add in any other seasoning desired. If using a Stockpot, bring to a boil and then reduce to simmer for 12 hours. Strain out the bones and any seasonings. Retain the bone broth.

Optional seasoning: Peppercorns, celery stalk & leaves, parsley, onion, cloves of garlic, turmeric, or ginger root.

- I drink it plain.
- Exchange for water when cooking rice or quinoa, and as a base for soups.
- Freezes well. Divide it into 2 cup servings for ease of use and storage space.

meats

Bacon

*Be sure to only use bacon that is nitrate-free, nitrite-free, and does not have added sugar.
The ingredients label should read only organic pork and salt.
My favorite way to cook bacon is in the oven. It reduces mess and pain from rogue oil spits!*

TIP

Retain the rendered bacon grease in a glass jar with a lid in the refrigerator and use it in place of avocado or olive oil for recipes.

INSTRUCTIONS

Line a rimmed sheet pan with parchment paper. Place the desired amount of bacon in one layer on the sheet pan and place the sheet pan in the cold oven. Turn on the oven to 300°F for thin/regular sliced bacon or 350°F for thick-sliced bacon (If you are unsure of the thickness, start with a lower temperature). Cook for 15 minutes and then flip the bacon. Return to the oven and cook for an additional 15 minutes. Check for the desired crispness level. Remove from the oven when desired crispness is achieved.

More for the Carnivore

Shrimp & Veggie Brown Rice Ramen

INGREDIENTS

2 cups shrimp, peeled, deveined
1 medium onion, chopped
4 cloves of garlic, chopped
1 cup broccoli, cut into florets
6 stalks asparagus, sliced
8-oz. of baby portabella mushrooms, sliced
½ cup baby tomatoes
2 cups fresh spinach, packed
2 Tbsp. grass-fed butter
2 Tbsp. olive oil
½ cup dry white wine
1 tsp. sea salt
1 tsp. black pepper
1 tsp. italian seasonings
Brown rice ramen noodles or raw zoodles

INSTRUCTIONS

Boil a pot of salted water. Cook noodles per instructions. While noodles are cooking, proceed with shrimp. In a saute pan, heat olive oil and "sauté" asparagus, mushrooms, and broccoli for a few minutes and then add the chopped onion. Move vegetables to the side, add the shrimp, and sprinkle with sea salt and pepper. Flip the shrimp after 2-3 minutes. Add diced garlic, butter, and white wine. Simmer for a few minutes. Add tomatoes and spinach and lower the temperature, cover and allow the spinach to wilt. Stir after a few minutes. Remove from heat and stir in cooked brown rice noodles or raw zoodles.

Frozen: Speed up the process by using frozen shrimp, broccoli, and spinach.

meats

Carnitas

INGREDIENTS

1 (4 lb.) pork shoulder, trimmed and cut into 2-inch pieces
2+ Tbsp. avocado oil
1 (12-oz.) beer (Pilsner or lager)
1 cup fresh squeezed orange juice
½ cup lime juice
7-9 cloves of garlic, chopped
2 tsp. sea salt
2 tsp. black pepper
2 tsp. chili powder
1 tsp. onion powder
1 tsp. dried oregano
1 tsp. ground cumin

Season the pork with sea salt and pepper.

> If using bone-in roast, save the bone for Collard Greens-pg. 85 & Bone Broth recipes-pg. 106
>
> Serve with Coconut Lime Cauliflower Rice-pg. 97, Spicy Squash-pg. 95, and Spicy Black Bean Dip-pg. 132

INSTRUCTIONS

 Turn on the Instapot and press the "sauté" button. Heat 1 Tbsp. of avocado oil and evenly brown the pork in batches for 3-4 minutes per side. When browned, remove from pot and cancel the Instapot. Add beer and juices to instapot and stir to release the stuck bits from the bottom. Stir in remaining ingredients and return the pork to the Instapot. Close and seal lid. Cook on high for 60 minutes. Allow pressure to release naturally for 15 minutes. Remove pork. Reduce the liquid on "sauté" mode for 5 minutes.

 Heat a large skillet over medium-high heat and add oil. When oil is hot, add in meat. Brown all sides of the meat, don't cook it all the way. Add the seasonings, beer, and juices and bring to a boil. Cover loosely and reduce heat to a low simmer. Stir every hour until the meat begins to fall apart. A cast iron skillet over gas heat distributes heat more evenly and reduces cooking time.

While the liquid is cooking, shred the pork. Return the shredded pork to the liquid and mix well. Turn on the broiler and set the top rack about 6 inches below. Transfer the meat to a baking sheet lined with aluminum foil and spread out evenly. Drizzle a few spoonfuls of the remaining liquid over the meat. Broil for 3-4 minutes until the meat starts to brown, remove the tray and flip the meat over. Return to the oven and brown for another 3-4 minutes. Remove from the oven and drizzle with remaining cooking liquid.

More for the Carnivore

Instapot Chuck Roast

INGREDIENTS

2-2½ lb. chuck roast
2 Tbsp. avocado oil
Sea salt and fresh ground pepper
1 cup beef broth
⅓ cup dry red wine
1 medium onion, chopped
6 cloves of garlic, chopped
1 tsp. paprika powder
1 tsp. ginger powdered
1 tsp. dried thyme
1 tsp. dried oregano
1 tsp. dried rosemary
4 carrots cut into 1½-2-inch segments

INSTRUCTIONS

Turn Instapot to "sauté" mode and heat the avocado oil. Brown roast on all sides and season with sea salt and pepper. Continue to rotate the roast until all sides are browned. Add onion, broth, red wine, and dried herbs, saving cloves of garlic until the end. Place the lid on and select "manual" mode setting for timer for 50 minutes. When the cooking time has ended, allow steam to release naturally for 10 minutes.

Once the steam has been released naturally on the Instapot, open the lid and add the carrots and cloves of garlic. Replace the lid and select "manual" for 3 minutes. Once the timer ends, allow steam to escape naturally for 10 minutes. Then shred beef with two forks.

TIP

- Serve with Cauliflower Mash-pg. 86 or quinoa

meats

Slow Cooker Salsa Chicken

This versatile recipe is very simple.

INGREDIENTS

4 chicken breasts
4 cloves of garlic, peeled
1 jar of salsa, select your desired heat level
1 jalapeño, diced

INSTRUCTIONS

Add the chicken breasts, salsa, and diced jalapeño, if using, to the slow cooker. Cook the chicken on low for 8 hours. The chicken will shred easily and be deliciously moist.

- I serve this chicken dish with cauliflower rice, Spicy Guacamole-pg. 136, and my Spicy Black Bean Dip- pg. 132 for a healthy and delicious Mexican themed dinner. Ole!

Bolognese Sauce

INGREDIENTS

1 lb. ground meat
2 Tbsp. avocado oil, divided
1 tsp. red pepper flakes or 1 jalapeño, diced
½ tsp. sea salt
1 medium onion, diced
4-6 cloves of garlic, minced
1 stalk celery, diced
1 carrot, grated
8-oz. baby bella mushrooms, diced
1 zucchini or summer squash, grated
28-oz. can crushed tomatoes or tomato sauce (ensure there is no added sugar)
8 fresh basil leaves, roughly chopped

INSTRUCTIONS

Heat 1 Tbsp. avocado oil over medium-high heat in a large skillet. Cook the meat with the sea salt, red pepper flakes, or jalapeño, stirring often, until brown and crumbly. Remove from the pan. Add the 2nd Tbsp. of avocado oil to the skillet and heat over medium-high heat. Add onion and mushrooms; "sauté" until tender, about 8-10 minutes. Add the garlic, celery, carrot, zucchini, and summer squash and "sauté" for 5 minutes. Mix the cooked meat back in, add the basil, canned tomatoes, or tomato sauce and cook over medium-low heat until the sauce thickens; around 10 minutes if using tomato sauce or around 30 minutes for canned tomatoes. Serve over raw zoodles, cooked spaghetti squash, or gluten-free pasta and top with parmesan cheese, optional.

- Omit the meat for a vegan variation. If meat is omitted, double mushrooms, squash, and increase other vegetables as desired.
- Beef and spicy Italian sausage are my favorites, but you can use bison, lamb, turkey, or any combination.
- Serve over raw zoodles, spaghetti squash, or gluten-free pasta and top with parmesan cheese.

Veggie Packed Meatloaf

Simple, quick, easy, delicious, and nutritious.

INGREDIENTS

2 Tbsp. avocado oil
2 lbs. of ground meat
1 small onion, chopped
4 cups chopped assorted vegetables
1 jalapeño
1 Tbsp. italian seasoning
4 cloves of garlic, chopped
2 organic eggs
1 tsp. Worcestershire sauce
½ tsp. sea salt
½ tsp. pepper
½ cup almond flour
2 Tbsp. of mustard

INSTRUCTIONS

Preheat the oven to 350°F. Process all the vegetables in the food processor or shred by hand. "Sauté" on medium-high heat, all vegetables and fresh garlic in avocado oil, season with sea salt, pepper, and Italian seasoning until softened. Remove as much liquid as possible. Combine vegetable mixture with all remaining ingredients with them together in a large bowl. Place into a greased loaf pan and cook for approximately 60 minutes until internal temperature reaches 165°F. Apply topping for the last 10-15 minutes.

Meat: use any combination of turkey, beef, pork, sausage, lamb, or bison. My favorite is a mix of 1 lb. each ground beef and hot italian sausage.

- My favorite vegetables: zucchini, yellow squash, bell peppers, mushrooms, carrots, and jalepeno.
- Try using a food processor.
- Place a sheet pan under the loaf pan as the liquid often drips over.
- Use a muffin tin for individual servings. Cook for 35-45 minutes.
- Serve with a side of Roasted Veggies-pg. 78 and Cauliflower Mash-pg. 86

Sausage, Cabbage, & Sweet Potatoes

*This recipe will not win any awards in a beauty pageant,
but it is very tasty, reheats well, and is delicious the next day!*

INGREDIENTS

1 lb. ground sausage
1 medium sweet potato, chopped
2-3 Tbsp. avocado oil or bacon grease
1 medium onion, chopped
1 medium/small purple head of cabbage, roughly chopped
4 cloves of garlic, diced
2 tsp. dried thyme
Salt and pepper, to taste
2 Tbsp. raw apple cider vinegar

INSTRUCTIONS

Heat 1 Tbsp. of oil in a cast iron skillet. Brown sausage for a few minutes. Add sweet potatoes and stir. Cover and heat until sweet potatoes start to soften. Add onion and stir, adding in more oil if needed, return cover. After onion softens, add cabbage, thyme, sea salt, pepper, and garlic, stir and cover. Cook for about 5-7 minutes. Remove from heat and add apple cider vinegar, stirring well to remove browned bits from the pan.

meats

Chicken Curry Soup

INGREDIENTS

1-2 Tbsp. avocado oil
1½ lb. boneless, skinless chicken thighs, cut into 1-inch chunks, smaller is better
1 tsp. sea salt
1 tsp. black pepper
1 tsp. cumin
1 tsp. cayenne
1 tsp. turmeric
4-6 cloves of garlic, diced
1 onion, diced
3 Tbsp. red curry paste (do not omit)
1 Tbsp. freshly grated ginger
6 cups of chicken or Bone Broth-pg. 106
1 can full-fat coconut milk
2 ramen rice noodles cakes (1-2 cakes per person; cooked per package instructions)
Chopped fresh cilantro and basil leaves
½ avocado, diced

INSTRUCTIONS

Heat oil in a Dutch oven or large stainless pot over medium heat. Season chicken with sea salt, pepper, cumin, cayenne, and turmeric. Cook chicken for 2-3 minutes, stirring until all sides are lightly cooked and remove from the pot. Cook onion until tender, 3-4 minutes. Stir in red curry paste, ginger, and garlic, for about 1 minute. Stir in broth and coconut milk. Be sure to scrape the goodies off the bottom of the pot. Add chicken and bring to a boil; reduce heat and cook for 10 minutes. Add rice noodles and cook per package instructions. Remove from heat and scoop out noodles from pot and place into two bowls, add more soup to the desired level, top with fresh herbs and diced avocado.

- Ensure all noodles are removed prior to storing as they will become soggy otherwise.
- Freezes well.
- For leftovers, reheat until simmering and cook a fresh batch of noodles for 3-5 minutes. Spoon into bowls and top with fresh herbs and diced avocado.

Chicken Zoodle Soup

INGREDIENTS

1 whole chicken (or at least 2 chicken carcasses with some remaining meat) including the organ meats (optional)
2 chicken livers (in addition to what came with the whole chicken; optional)
2 beef bones with cartilage, meat, and/or marrow included
5 large carrots, chopped
1 large onion, chopped
3 ribs of celery, chopped
1 Tbsp. black peppercorns
1 Tbsp. sea salt
1 Tbsp. raw apple cider vinegar
½ bundle of parsley (stems and leaves roughly chopped)

Water (amount depends on the number of bones and amount of meat used)

5-8 cloves of garlic, crushed (add at the last few minutes of cooking)

INSTRUCTIONS

Zoodles:
3 raw zucchini, spiralized or chopped in preferred size and shape

Prepare the stock by adding the beef bones, whole chicken or chicken bones and organ meats, celery, carrot, onion, sea salt, black peppercorns, and apple cider vinegar to the soup pot and cover contents with water. Bring to a boil, then reduce heat to low. After 3 hours, let cool for an hour or more with the lid off. Strain. Reserve the meat from the bones and the broth only. Divide broth into two batches. One for now and one for later.

Two options:
1. Add back in the chicken, liver, and carrot mixture, along with the spiralized zucchini. Simmer for 30 minutes, adding in the garlic in the last 10 minutes before turning the burner off. Season with sea salt to taste.

2. Keep the stock, chicken, and raw zoodles separate. Combine and heat in small batches as needed. I typically keep it separate and then heat up just what we need throughout the week.

These bones have been cooked well and will likely not make a good batch of bone broth after being used in this soup recipe. Therefore, discard the bones after using them.

Beef Stew

INGREDIENTS

4 lbs. chuck roast, cubed
2-3 beef soup bones
72-oz. tomato puree
5 carrots, sliced
2 onions, diced
1 lb. peas, frozen
1 squash, zucchini, or a mix, diced
6 cloves of garlic, crushed
2 Tbsp. sea salt
1 Tbsp. raw apple cider vinegar

INSTRUCTIONS

Add all ingredients to the pot, with the exception of the garlic, and bring to a boil. Reduce heat to low and cover, cooking for 3 to 4 hours, until the meat is tender. Remember to add garlic 5 minutes before the end of cooking time.

- Remove soup bones and discard or freeze for a batch of bone broth.
- Serve with a side of Cauliflower Mash-pg. 86

Beef & Cabbage Soup

INGREDIENTS

2 Tbsp. avocado oil or bacon grease
1 large onion, chopped
1 lb. grass-fed rib-eye steak or stew meat, cut into 1-inch pieces
1 stalk celery, chopped
2 large carrots, diced
1 small green cabbage, chopped
4 cloves of garlic, minced
3 cups Bone Broth-pg. 106
3 Tbsp. fresh parsley, chopped
2 Tbsp. fresh rosemary, chopped
2 tsp. onion and garlic powder
Salt and black pepper to taste

INSTRUCTIONS

Heat oil or grease in a large pot over medium heat, add the beef and sear on all sides until browned all over (it does not need to be cooked through). Then add the onions and cook until transparent, about 3-4 minutes. Add the celery and carrots to the pan. Cook for about 3-4 minutes, stirring occasionally, then add the cabbage and cook for 5 minutes until beginning to soften. Add the stock or broth, garlic, rosemary, parsley, dried herbs, and onion and garlic powder, mixing well. Reduce heat to a simmer and cover. Allow to simmer for 10-15 minutes, or until the cabbage and carrots are soft. Serve warm with a sprinkle of fresh parsley.

- This soup can be refrigerated once cooled in airtight containers for up to 3 days, or frozen for up to 2 months.

Beef & Broccoli Stir Fry

INGREDIENTS

2 Tbsp. avocado oil, divided
4 cups broccoli florets
2 cloves of garlic, minced
1 lb. grass-fed flank steak or steak tips, thinly sliced

Sauce and Marinade:
⅓ cup coconut aminos
¼ cup chicken broth
1 Tbsp. avocado oil
1 tsp. ground ginger
¼ tsp. cayenne
1 Tbsp. unflavored grass-fed gelatin powder

Serve with:
- Cauliflower rice, cooked
- Quinoa (use Bone Broth- pg. 106)

INSTRUCTIONS

In a small bowl, whisk together the coconut aminos, ground ginger, and cayenne. Transfer 2 Tbsp. of this mixture to a large bowl and whisk in 1 Tbsp. of avocado oil. Add the beef to this large bowl, ensure all surfaces are coated, and place in the refrigerator for 30 minutes. Heat 1 Tbsp. avocado oil in a "sauté" pan over medium-high heat. Add beef and cook for a few minutes until browned on all sides. Remove the beef, place in a bowl, and cover to keep warm.

Heat the remaining 1 Tbsp. of avocado oil over medium heat. Add the broccoli, cover with a lid for 8-12 minutes, occasionally lifting to stir, until crispy and tender. Remove the broccoli and place it in the bowl with the beef. Whisk the chicken broth and gelatin into the initial sauce (not the marinade that was used for the beef). Add the gelatin slowly, sprinkling it over while stirring to prevent clumping. Heat the pan again over medium heat, add the garlic, and "sauté" for 1 minute. Pour the sauce into the pan and simmer, occasionally stirring, for about 5 minutes, until it starts to thicken and reduce. Add beef and broccoli to the pan, toss to coat, and stir for another few minutes until hot.

sheet pan deliciousness
Sausage, Brussels Sprouts, Sweet Potatoes, & Apples

INGREDIENTS

12-oz. Brussels sprouts, halved
1 large or 2 medium sweet potatoes, diced
1 granny smith, gala, or pink lady apple, chopped (select the variety that is in-season and has the desired sweetness level)
3–4 chicken apple sausages, thickly sliced
3 Tbsp. avocado oil
1 tsp. dried thyme
Dash of garlic powder
Dash of onion powder
Salt and pepper
Fresh rosemary sprigs
¼ tsp cayenne pepper (optional)

INSTRUCTIONS

Preheat the oven to 400°F and line a baking sheet with parchment paper. In a large bowl, toss the Brussels sprouts, squash, chopped apple, sliced sausage, and avocado oil. Spread the vegetable and sausage mix on the pan. Season with the thyme, garlic, onion, sea salt, pepper, and cayenne. Lay 3-4 rosemary springs down on the pan. Bake for about 35 minutes, until the vegetables are fork-tender and browned. Serve immediately.

- This dish can be served on its own or it pairs well with Cauliflower Mash-pg. 86

Sausage: I prefer Aidell's or Applegate brand.

meats

sheet pan deliciousness

Sweet Italian Sausage & Veggies

INGREDIENTS

1 pack (4) sweet Italian sausage
½ head of cauliflower cut into florets
2-4 Tbsp. avocado oil
1 Tbsp. ghee (optional)
16-20 asparagus spears, with tough ends removed
3-4 Tbsp. nutritional yeast
2 tsp. sea salt

INSTRUCTIONS

Preheat the oven to 400°F. Line two sheet pans with parchment paper and drizzle with avocado oil. On one sheet pan, start cauliflower florets first and cook for 25 minutes or until starting to brown. On the second sheet pan, line up sausages and place in the oven. When the timer ends, flip cauliflower and return to the oven. Flip sausages over, add asparagus and buffalo ghee, if using, to the sausage sheet pan, and return to the oven. Cook all for an additional 20-25 minutes until fully cooked and browned. Sprinkle sea salt and nutritional yeast on cauliflower, stir to cover.

Alternative cooking fats: rendered bacon grease or avocado oil

Sausage: I purchase from Butcher's Box or Whole Foods.

More for the Carnivore

sheet pan deliciousness

Chicken Sausage, Potatoes, & Broccoli

INGREDIENTS

1 pack of chicken sausage
2 large or 3 medium potatoes, peeled and sliced
1 bunch of broccoli, chopped into florets
2 Tbsp. avocado oil
1-2 tsp. sea salt

INSTRUCTIONS

Peel and thinly slice potatoes. Drizzle with avocado oil and place on the sheet pan lined with parchment paper. Cook at 400°F for 25 minutes. While the potatoes are cooking, prepare the broccoli. Chop broccoli into equal-sized florets. Place on the sheet pan with potatoes, drizzle with avocado oil and sprinkle with sea salt. Then add the sausages to the sheet pan and return the sheet pan to the oven. Cook for another 25 minutes or until everything is as crispy as desired. Remember to cook less if the potatoes are sliced thin.

Potatoes: thinner slices will be crispier but be cautious not to cut them too thin or they will burn

meats

sheet pan deliciousness

Oven-Baked Boneless Chicken Thighs

INGREDIENTS

6-8 skinless, boneless chicken thighs
2 Tbsp. paprika
1 Tbsp. garlic powder
1 Tbsp. onion powder
1 Tbsp. dried thyme
2 tsp. sea salt
2-3 Tbsp. avocado oil

INSTRUCTIONS

Preheat the oven to 425°F. Mix all the dry spices in a large bowl. Dredge chicken thighs in the spices, covering all sides. Place parchment paper on a baking sheet. Lay chicken thighs on the baking sheet. Drizzle with the avocado oil. Cook for 20-30 minutes, flipping halfway, or until chicken is cooked through and reads 165°F internally.

- Serve with a side of Roasted Veggies-pg. 78 and Cauliflower Mash-pg. 86

sheet pan deliciousness

Indian Spiced Baked Chicken

INGREDIENTS

6-8 skinless, boneless chicken thighs
1 Tbsp. cumin powder
½ Tbsp. cayenne powder
1 Tbsp. turmeric powder
2 tsp. sea salt
1 tsp. ground black pepper
2-3 Tbsp. bacon grease or avocado oil

INSTRUCTIONS

Preheat the oven to 425°F. Place 2-3 Tbsp. bacon grease on a sheet pan lined with parchment paper. Heat for a few minutes until melted. Place chicken thighs on the sheet pan and coat each side with the melted bacon grease; if using avocado oil, omit this step and simply drizzle on the chicken thighs. Sprinkle both sides with sea salt, cumin, chili pepper, cayenne, turmeric, and black pepper. Cook for 15 minutes and then flip.

- Serve with a side of Roasted Veggies-pg. 78 and Cauliflower Mash-pg. 86

meats

sheet pan deliciousness

Oven-Baked Chicken Drumsticks

INGREDIENTS

5-6 chicken drumsticks
1 Tbsp. paprika
1 Tbsp. garlic powder
1 Tbsp. onion powder
1 Tbsp. cayenne
1 Tbsp. cinnamon (do not omit)
2 tsp. sea salt
1 tsp. black pepper
2-3 Tbsp. bacon grease or avocado oil

INSTRUCTIONS

Preheat the oven to 425°F. Mix all the dry spices in a large bowl. Dredge chicken drumsticks in the spices, covering all sides. Place parchment paper on a rimmed baking sheet. Lay chicken drumsticks on the baking sheet. Drizzle with bacon grease or avocado oil. Cook for 40-50 minutes, flipping halfway, or until chicken is cooked through and reads 165°F internally and skin is crispy.

- Serve with a side of Roasted Veggies-pg. 78 and Cauliflower Mash-pg. 86

More for the Carnivore

Dijon Salmon

INGREDIENTS

1 ½ lbs. salmon filet
1 Tbsp. dijon mustard
2 Tbsp. lemon juice
3 Tbsp. fresh parsley, chopped
3 cloves of garlic, roughly chopped
2 Tbsp. olive oil
½ tsp. sea salt
½ tsp. pepper

INSTRUCTIONS

Preheat the oven to 450°F and line a baking sheet with foil (I rarely advise the use of foil over parchment paper, but with the high temperature of this recipe foil is preferable). Slice the salmon into pieces and sprinkle the skin with sea salt (to aid in removing the skin after cooking). Combine the dijon mustard, lemon juice, parsley, garlic, olive oil, sea salt, and pepper in a small bowl. Generously spread the marinade all over the salmon. Bake for 12-15 minutes or until just cooked through. Be very cautious not to overcook.

- Serve with a side of Sheet Pan Roasted Veggies-pg. 78 and Cauliflower Mash-pg. 86

Low-Cook Salmon

meats

INGREDIENTS

1-1 ½ lbs. salmon filet
2 tsp. sea salt
2 tsp. black pepper
2 Tbsp. lemon juice
2 Tbsp. olive oil
2-4 cloves of garlic, chopped
4 sprigs fresh rosemary or parsley or both, chopped

INSTRUCTIONS

Preheat the oven to 300°F and line a baking sheet with parchment paper. Sprinkle 1 tsp. of sea salt on the skin side of the salmon (to aid in removing the skin after cooking). Place salmon on the baking sheet and drizzle lemon juice and olive oil. Sprinkle with sea salt, pepper, and fresh chopped herbs of choice. Bake until the salmon releases its fat (it will look like white streaks) and flakes easily, about 20-25 minutes depending on the thickness of the salmon and your oven. Serve immediately.

- Serve with a side of Roasted Veggies-pg. 78 and Cauliflower Mash-pg. 86!

My Favorite Herbs: Cilantro, parsley, and rosemary; diced cloves of garlic and grated fresh ginger root

More for the Carnivore

Shrimp Stir Fry

This is a fast paced recipe. Have everything chopped, mixed, prepared and ready to go before you start cooking.

INGREDIENTS

1 lb. shrimp, peeled and deveined
2 Tbsp. avocado oil
2 cups fresh or frozen broccoli florets
1 tsp. red pepper flakes
1 tsp. ground ginger
½ cup carrots, shredded
8-oz. of baby portabella mushrooms, sliced
1 cup snow peas
1 cup bell peppers, sliced
1 tsp. fresh ginger root, grated
2 cloves of garlic, diced

SAUCE:
2 Tbsp. rice vinegar or raw apple cider vinegar
¼ cup of coconut amino
1-2 tsp. chili garlic sauce, sriracha, or favorite hot sauce
1 tsp. raw honey
2 tsp. sesame oil

INSTRUCTIONS

Heat the avocado oil in a large cast-iron skillet or "sauté" pan. Cook the broccoli for about 5 minutes and remove it. Sauté the shrimp along with the red pepper flakes, ground ginger, and sea salt for 3-4 minutes. Add in the rest of the vegetables: carrots, mushrooms, snow peas, and bell peppers. Sauté for 3-4 minutes and then add broccoli back in for another 5 minutes. While the vegetables are cooking, make the sauce. Add in the diced garlic and grated ginger root to the sautéing vegetables. Stir in the sauce for the last 1-2 minutes. Serve immediately over cauliflower rice (or brown rice ramen or raw zoodles) and top with garnishes of your choice.

Serve with:
- 2-3 cups cauliflower rice, cooked
- Brown rice ramen noodles
- Raw zoodles

Optional Garnishes:
- Scallions, diced
- Sesame seeds
- Jalapeño, diced, remove seeds for less heat

BEFORE, IN BETWEEN, & AFTER

Spicy Black Bean Dip

Classic Hummus

Cilantro Lime Hummus

Spicy Avocado Hummus

Spicy Guacamole

Roasted Chickpeas–5 Ways

Cucumber Goat Cheese Bites

snacks +

Keep raw fresh vegetables on hand for quick, healthy snacks alone, with nut butter, or with one of the delicious dips in this book. Some of my favorites include carrots, celery, snow peas, green beans, broccoli*, cauliflower*, bell peppers**, and baby tomatoes**. The vegetables are full of phytonutrients and fiber which are better absorbed when paired with healthy fats, like those found in one of these healthy dips.

*If you have a thyroid disorder, be sure to cook or steam the brassica family vegetables before eating them. These include broccoli, cauliflower, Brussels sprouts, and cabbage.

**For thyroid disorder, an inflammatory, or autoimmune disease avoid nightshade vegetables. These include tomatoes, potatoes, eggplant, and peppers.

 **SMART INGREDIENTS**

Sea Salt: Pink Himalayan sea salt or Grey Celtic sea salt

Spicy Black Bean Dip

INGREDIENTS

2 cups cooked black beans
½-¾ cup salsa
1 jalapeño (optional)
¼-½ cup cilantro, chopped
2 Tbsp. lime juice
1-2 cloves of garlic, chopped
1 tsp. cumin
1 tsp. granulated garlic
1 tsp. cayenne powder (optional)

INSTRUCTIONS

Add all ingredients to the blender and blend until smooth. Serve with corn or tortilla chips.

- I prefer medium heat salsa.
- Delicious when served with carrots and celery.
- Use as a topping for Buddha Bowl-pg. 78, Carnitas Bowls-pg. 109, or in the Collard Green Wraps-pg. 84

Classic Hummus

INGREDIENTS

⅓ cup tahini
2 Tbsp. cold water (you may need to add 2-3 Tbsp. more)
2 Tbsp. olive oil
½ tsp. ground cumin
¾ tsp. sea salt
4 cloves of garlic, peeled
2 Tbsp. lemon juice or the juice of 1 lemon
1 can chickpea, drained and rinsed

INSTRUCTIONS

Add all ingredients to the food processor except the chickpeas. Puree until smooth. Add the chickpeas and puree for 3-4 minutes. Add more water if the mixture seems too thick and scrape down the sides as needed. Taste and add additional sea salt, cumin, and/or lemon juice, as needed.

- Delicious when served with carrots and celery.
- Use as a topping for a Buddha Bowl-pg. 78 or in the Collard Green Wraps-pg. 84

Cilantro Lime Hummus

INGREDIENTS

Start with the Classic Hummus recipe-pg. 133
Omit the lemon juice and add:

2 Tbsp. organic lime juice or the juice of 1 lime

15-20 sprigs of fresh organic cilantro (include both leaves and stems)

INSTRUCTIONS

Add all ingredients to the food processor, except the chickpeas. Puree until smooth. Add the chickpeas and puree for 3-4 minutes. Add more water if the mixture seems too thick and scrape down the sides as needed. Taste and add additional sea salt, cumin, and/or lime juice as needed.

- Delicious when served with carrots and celery
- Use as a topping for a Buddha Bowl-pg. 78 or in the Collard Green Wraps-pg. 84

Spicy Avocado Hummus

INGREDIENTS

Start with the Classic Hummus recipe-pg. 133. Omit the tahini and lemon juice and add:

1 lg. or 2 sm. ripe avocados

2 Tbsp. lime juice or the juice of 1 lime

15-20 sprigs of fresh cilantro sprigs (include both leaves and stems)

½-1 jalapeño (remove the seeds if you want mild flavor or add the entire jalapeño if you prefer more heat)

INSTRUCTIONS

Add all ingredients to the food processor, except the chickpeas. Puree until smooth. Add the chickpeas and puree for 3-4 minutes. Add more water if the mixture seems too thick and scrape down the sides as needed. Taste and add additional sea salt, cumin, and/or lime juice as needed.

- Delicious when served with carrots and celery
- Use as a topping for a Buddha Bowl-pg. 78 or in the Collard Green Wraps-pg. 84

Spicy Guacamole

INGREDIENTS

2 large ripe avocados
2 tsp. lime juice
¼ cup red or white onion, finely chopped
½-1 jalapeño (seed and rib removed, finely chopped or add the whole jalapeño for more heat)
2 Tbsp. fresh cilantro, finely chopped
½ tsp. sea salt
¼ tsp. ground cumin

INSTRUCTIONS

Cut avocados in half, remove seeds (retaining one for leftovers), and scoop out the flesh.

Option 1: Place avocado into a large bowl. Mash with a fork until smooth. Add all the remaining ingredients. Stir and taste. Add more ingredients to your preference.

Option 2: For smoother guacamole, chop the cilantro and jalapeño finer and add all ingredients to a food processor. Process until desired consistency.

- Keep 1 avocado seed to place in leftovers to prevent browning.
- Serve chilled, for at least 20 minutes before serving.
- Serve with the Buddha Bowl-pg. 78, Carnitas Bowl-pg. 109, in the Collard Greens Wraps-pg. 84 or with carrots and celery sticks.

snacks +

Roasted Chickpeas - 5 Ways

Quick and savory protein-packed snacks.

INGREDIENTS

1 can of chickpeas, rinsed
2 tsp. sea salt
2 Tbsp. avocado oil

INSTRUCTIONS

Mix the ingredients and roast on a rimmed baking sheet at 450°F for 20 minutes.
Eat plain or add in the following ingredients for delicious twists:

Spiced Maple
1 tsp. paprika
¼ tsp. cayenne
1 tsp. chili powder
¼ cup raw maple syrup

Turmeric & Lime
½ tsp. ginger powder
2 tsp. turmeric
½ tsp. black pepper
Juice from 1 lime (2 Tbsp.)

"Parmesan Cheese"
2 Tbsp. nutritional yeast
1 tsp. olive oil

Ranch
½ tsp. dried thyme
1 tsp. onion powder
1 tsp. dried dill
½ tsp. garlic powder
½ tsp. black pepper

Cucumber Goat Cheese Bites

INGREDIENTS

1 English cucumber, sliced into ¼-inch rounds
Goat cheese (the amount depends on the size of your cucumber)
¼ tsp. sea salt
½ tsp. paprika

INSTRUCTIONS

Cut the cucumber into rounds and lay flat. Place a small piece of goat cheese on each slice. You may need to massage the cheese to fit nicely on the cucumber. Sprinkle with sea salt and paprika!

SWEET TREATS

Coconut Whipped Cream

Chocolate Peanut Butter Protein Bites

Almond Coconut Protein Bites

Pot de Crème

Cacao Pudding

Cacao Banana 'Ice Cream'

Avocado Banana Chocolate Pudding

Chocolate and Peanut Butter Chia Pudding

sweetness

As discussed in the beginning, refined white sugar is dangerous for our health and is put into a lot of processed foods without our knowledge. It is critical to avoid refined white sugar. I utilize natural sweeteners that contain numerous health benefits like raw honey, pure maple syrup, and fruit, like dried dates, to add sweetness to my recipes.

 **SMART INGREDIENTS**

Sea Salt: Pink Himalayan sea salt or Grey Celtic sea salt.

Canned Ccoconut Milk & Cream: Full fat. Check that there are no added thickeners, sweeteners, or gums and it is in a BPA-free can.

Chocolate: 70% cocoa content. Be sure to check the label to ensure there are no added sugars.

Protein Powder: I use *Designs for Health PurePaleo* and *Orgain Organic Protein* plant-based powders.

Chocolate Chips: I use gluten, dairy, nut, and soy-free chocolate chips brand Enjoy Life.

MCT Oil: Use C8 oil only, which is the potent oil within coconut oil that converts directly to energy; I use Designs for Health KTO-C8-100.

Coconut Whipped Cream

INGREDIENTS

1 can coconut cream
1 tsp. of vanilla extract

INSTRUCTIONS

Place the can of coconut cream in the refrigerator overnight to allow the milk fats to solidify. Place the mixing bowl and beater in the freezer for at least 10 minutes. Open the can and drain out the liquid part reserving the solid creamy milk fat (save the liquid part to drink or add to smoothies). Place the milk solids in a large mixing bowl and beat with a mixer until light and fluffy. Add the vanilla extract and mix until well combined.

- Delicious served over a bowl of fresh berries or on top of Cacao Pudding-pg. 146, Chocolate and Peanut Butter Chia Pudding-pg. 149, and Pot de Crème-pg. 145

sweet treats

Chocolate Peanut Butter Protein Bites

INGREDIENTS

1½ cups gluten-free, old-fashioned rolled oats
1 cup natural peanut butter
1-2 Tbsp. MCT or raw coconut oil
¼ cup raw honey
2 scoops (about 50–60 grams) chocolate protein powder
2 Tbsp. chocolate chips (optional)

INSTRUCTIONS

Place ingredients in a large bowl and stir to combine. Getting the mixture to combine takes a little arm muscle and it may seem too thick at first, but it will come together as you keep mixing (I used my hands to knead the dough near the end and that seems to help). Once combined, use a small cookie scooper to form the dough into balls. Store in a covered container in the fridge or in the freezer in a container lined with parchment paper.

Peanut Butter: If I want some crunch, I use a combination of NuttZo nut butter – cashew, almond, brazil nut, flaxseed, chia seed, hazelnuts, and pumpkin seeds along with natural peanut butter.

Sweetness

Almond Coconut Protein Bites

INGREDIENTS

1½ cups gluten-free, old-fashioned rolled oats
1 cup natural almond butter
1-2 Tbsp. MCT or raw coconut oil
¼ cup raw honey
2 scoops (about 50–60 grams) chocolate protein powder
1-2 Tbsp. unsweetened shredded coconut

INSTRUCTIONS

Place ingredients in a large bowl and stir to combine. Getting the mixture to combine takes a little arm muscle and it may seem too thick at first, but it will come together as you keep mixing (I used my hands to knead the dough near the end and that seems to help). Once combined, use a small cookie scooper to form the dough into balls. Store in a covered container in the fridge or in the freezer in a container lined with parchment paper.

sweet treats

Pot de Crème

INGREDIENTS

½ cup + 1 Tbsp. raw cacao powder or unsweetened dark 70+% cocoa powder
1 tsp. finely ground espresso or coffee
¾ cup chopped vegan bittersweet/dark chocolate
¼ tsp. sea salt
1 (14-oz.) can coconut milk, divided
1 tsp. vanilla exract
1-2 Tbsp. pure maple syrup
5-9 pitted dried dates

INSTRUCTIONS

In a small saucepan heated to medium-low, combine cocoa powder, espresso powder, cocoa butter, sea salt, and ¾ cup coconut milk. Whisk constantly until melted. Once melted, whisk in the remaining coconut milk and remove from heat. Whisk in the vanilla extract and maple syrup, to taste (remember that the dates will also add sweetness and if the chocolate used has added sugar, use less maple syrup). Transfer the mixture to a blender carefully as the mixture is hot. Add dates starting with 5 and increase to taste (I usually end up using all 9 especially if they are small) and blend on high until creamy and smooth. Transfer to individual cups or ramekins and wrap. Refrigerate until cold and thickened, at least 4 hours, but preferably overnight.

Optional Toppings:
- Coconut Whipped Cream-pg. 142
- 2-4 tsp. raw cacao nibs
- 1-2 tsp. raw cacao powder or 70% dark cocoa powder
- Keeps in the refrigerator for up to 7 days.

Sweetness

Cacao Pudding

INGREDIENTS

1 can coconut milk
½ cup dried pitted dates
¼ cup raw cacao powder
½ tsp. ground cinnamon
Pinch of sea salt
¼ cup chia seeds

INSTRUCTIONS

Combine coconut milk, dates, cacao powder, cinnamon, and sea salt in a blender or food processor and blend for about 1-2 minutes, until smooth. Pour the mixture into a medium bowl and stir in chia seeds. Allow to set in the refrigerator for at least 4 hours, ideally overnight. Serve in small bowls with coconut whipped cream and cacao nibs on top.

Optional Toppings:
- Coconut Whipped Cream-pg. 142
- 2-4 tsp. raw cacao nibs

sweet treats

Cacao Banana 'Ice Cream'

INGREDIENTS

1 frozen banana
½ Tbsp. raw cacao powder or unsweetened dark 70+% cocoa powder
½ Tbsp. nut butter

INSTRUCTIONS

Blend until mixed and freeze for at least 30 minutes.

- I make this ahead of time, place the mixture in a bowl, and freeze until dessert time.

Avocado Banana Chocolate Pudding

INGREDIENTS

2 avocados, peeled and pitted
1 banana (ideally not too ripe)
¼ cup raw cacao powder or unsweetened dark 70+% cocoa powder
1 Tbsp. raw honey
2 tsp. coconut oil

INSTRUCTIONS

Mix avocados, banana, cocoa powder, honey, and coconut oil in a blender. Puree until smooth. Pour into serving dishes. Chill in the refrigerator for 30 minutes. Enjoy immediately!

sweet treats

Chocolate & Peanut Butter Chia Pudding

INGREDIENTS

¼ cup chia seeds
1 cup nut milk
1 Tbsp. raw maple syrup
1 tsp. vanilla extract
Pinch of sea salt

Chocoate Layer:
2 Tbsp. raw cacao powder or unsweetened dark 70+% cocoa powder

Peanut Butter Layer:
½ cup sugar-free peanut butter (use less maple syrup if peanut butter contains sugar)

INSTRUCTIONS

Mix chia seeds and nut milk. Let sit for at least an hour in the refrigerator. Add the rest of the ingredients and process in the blender. Once each pudding is completed, layer the chocolate and peanut butter puddings alternating in a bowl. Serve chilled.

- I enjoy topping with raw cacao nibs and Coconut Whipped Cream-pg. 142
- As an alternative, you can make the chocolate or the peanut butter chia pudding alone, topped with coconut whipped cream and cacao nibs

Milk Alternatives: Choose from unsweetened coconut, hemp or almond milk.

Sweetness

BEVERAGES

Infused Water
Anti-Inflammatory Ginger Water
Electrolyte Replenishment
Mock-tails
Probiotic Beverages

beverages

Pure clean water is the ideal source for hydration. The majority of Americans are dehydrated. Drink a minimum of half your body weight (lbs.) in ounces, daily. For example: If you weigh 150 lbs., you should drink a minimum of 75-oz. of water daily. A delicious way to increase your hydration without increasing your waistline is with infused water.

 **SMART INGREDIENTS**

Sea Salt: Pink Himalayan sea salt or Grey Celtic sea salt.

Infused Water

INSTRUCTIONS

- Add a splash of organic lemon juice or organic lemon slices which also adds immune-boosting vitamin C
- Slices of fresh organic ginger root are anti-inflammatory
- Fresh organic mint leaves provide a refreshing taste
- Freeze organic mint leaves in an ice cube tray filled with organic pomegranate or tart cherry juice and add to soda water for a refreshing summer drink
- Organic cucumber slices and fresh organic mint leaves create a spa-like refreshing drink
- Organic berries like blackberries, raspberries, and/or sliced strawberries

Organic green tea, organic coffee, and espresso all have excellent antioxidant properties. Be certain you are consuming these products in the organic form only as the conventional forms have extremely high levels of pesticides.

Make your own ginger mint tea by simply slicing organic ginger root and adding to a mug with a few fresh organic mint leaves and steep in boiling water for 3-5 minutes. I often make a large batch and keep it in the refrigerator.

Anti-Inflammatory Ginger Infused Water

INGREDIENTS

1 (4-6-inch) piece of organic ginger root, sliced
6-8 cups of water

INSTRUCTIONS

Bring water to a boil in a large pot. Add the sliced ginger and reduce heat to simmer. Allow to simmer, uncovered, for 30-45 minutes or until about half the water content has evaporated. Store in a glass pitcher in the refrigerator.

For spicier water:
- Add more ginger
- Simmer longer (resulting in more concentrated liquid)
- Slice the ginger thinner
- Keep the ginger root in with the infused water in the glass pitcher

Optional Add-Ins:
- Slice an organic lemon and add to the chilled infused ginger water.

Electrolyte Replenishment

Strenuous exercise, summer heat, or illness require an increase in electrolyte intake, especially sodium, potassium, and trace minerals, which are found in sea salt. 100% pure, unsweetened, organic coconut water is a tasty source of electrolytes.

Here are three tasty electrolyte replacement beverage recipes.

INGREDIENTS

Tart Cherry Sport Drink
32 oz. of water
1 teaspoon sea salt
24 oz. of organic tart cherry juice
¼ cup organic lemon juice

Pina Colada Sport Drink
12-oz. of water
½ tsp. sea salt
32 oz. of coconut water
12 oz. of 100% organic pineapple juice
¼ cup organic lemon juice

Ginger Lemonade
32 oz. water
2-inch organic ginger root, sliced
Juice of 1 organic lemon or 2 Tbsp. organic lemon juice

INSTRUCTIONS

Combine ingredients in a large glass pitcher. Keep refrigerated and consume within 3 days.

drinks

Mock-Tails

INGREDIENTS

1-2 Tbsp. organic tart cherry juice or lemon juice
1 teaspoon organic lime juice
8-10 oz. of plain seltzer or mineral water

INSTRUCTIONS

Mix together and enjoy chilled.

Probiotic Beverages

These tasty beverages are full of immune-boosting healthy probiotics.

Water kefir and kombucha are relatively simple to make at home with kits you can buy online, but there are delicious versions that are available in most stores.

My favorite brand of water kefir is Sunny Culture which I buy from Whole Foods, my local farmers market, and online through my local organic delivery company, Red Tractor.

My favorite brand of kombucha is GT's which is sold at Publix, Whole Foods, and Costco.

Mylo's Dinner Bell

I use all organic ingredients for our sweet Mylo because we value his health.

Since Mylo is a little guy, about 11 lbs., this recipe is in Mylo sized portions. Doubling or tripling this recipe is simple to do for your larger sized pet. I recommend making a small batch first and adding it to their food for a few weeks to transition them, as some dogs have sensitive stomachs that may react negatively to sudden food changes.

This recipe includes the basic nutrition a healthy dog needs including protein, carbohydrates, fiber, essential vitamins, and minerals.

Puppies need about 25% protein and extra fat, so select a fattier cut of meat than for an adult dog who needs around 18% protein.

You can adjust the amount and type of meat based on your dog's age, activity level, and nutritional status.

doggie bag

INGREDIENTS
1 lb. ground turkey, chicken, pork, beef, or combination
1 Tbsp. olive oil
1 cup brown rice or quinoa (cooked per package instructions with water) or Mylo's favorite is 1 cup sweet potato (cooked and smashed, include the skin chopped into small pieces)
⅓ zucchini, shredded
1 carrot, shredded
1 cup fresh or frozen spinach leaves (packed and roughly chopped)
¼ cup fresh or frozen peas

INSTRUCTIONS
Heat the oil over medium heat. Add the ground meat, stir to break it apart, and cook until browned on all sides, about 5-7 minutes. Add the vegetables, stir and cook for a few minutes until soft. Allow to cool completely before serving. Keeps in the refrigerator for 5-7 days and in the freezer for 3 months.

- **Protein Alternatives:** Cooked boneless chicken breasts or thighs, organ meat, or de-boned fish cooked only in water or a small amount of oil. Do not add salt or any seasonings.
- **Carbohydrates/Vegetables/Fiber Alternatives:** Steamed sweet potatoes, pumpkin, squash, broccoli florets, or cooked oatmeal. Do not add salt or any seasonings.
- Mylo's favorite meat is beef. I select 75%/25% to give my little guy some extra healthy fat for puppy development.
- I use a food processor to speed up preparing the carrots and zuchinni.

For Your Furry Family Members

PART 3

LET'S GET HEALTHY!

IN THIS PART:

Shopping, Stocking, Prepping, & Cooking

Shopping Guides & Produce References

Dr. Anya's Quick Health Guide

References

14

Shopping, Stocking, Prepping, and Cooking

Stock up when there is a sale! Always purchase organic!

This is a list of the most commonly used ingredients for the recipes in this book. Focus on what is local and in-season. I purchase my pantry items from Costco, Thrive Market, and Whole Foods.

OILS
- [] Avocado
- [] Extra virgin olive

RAW NUTS
- [] Walnuts
- [] Pecans
- [] Macadamia

BUTTERS
- [] Peanut
- [] Almond
- [] Tahini

MILK
- [] Coconut
- [] Almond
- [] Hemp
- [] Canned coconut

OTHER
- [] Apple Cider Vinegar (Bragg's)
- [] Quinoa
- [] Canned chickpeas & black beans
- [] Raw cacao powder & nibs
- [] Vanilla extract
- [] Coconut aminos

RAW SEEDS
- [] Hemp
- [] Chia
- [] Sunflower
- [] Pumpkin
- [] Ground flax

Our bodies cannot digest whole flax seed

SWEETENERS
- [] Raw local honey
- [] Raw maple syrup
- [] Dried dates

SPICES

Buy in bulk from a natural grocery store like Sprouts or Whole Foods.

- [ ] Granulated garlic
- [ ] Paprika
- [ ] Black pepper
- [ ] Italian seasoning
- [ ] Cinnamon
- [ ] Ginger
- [ ] Turmeric
- [ ] Cayenne
- [ ] Cumin
- [ ] Curry

Shop for ORGANIC ingredients

PRODUCE

Local farmers market or find an organic produce delivery in your area. It will support your local organic farmers & economy.

Focus your purchases on what is local and in season.

- [ ] Berries & fruits
- [ ] Vegetables
- [ ] Bottled lemon juice
- [ ] Herbs
- [ ] Grass-fed salted butter

FROZEN

Great to have on hand for quick meal preps! Good deals at Costco and Whole Foods.

- [ ] Peas
- [ ] Broccoli florets
- [ ] Cauliflower florets/rice
- [ ] Shrimp

MEAT & EGGS

I purchase these items from my local farmers market, at Costco, and Whole Foods, or online from Butcher's Box, Moink, and 5 Mary's.

- [ ] Free-range eggs
- [ ] Nitrate-free, sugar-free bacon
- [ ] Grass-fed beef and bison
- [ ] Chicken sausage
- [ ] Chicken broth paste
- [ ] Wild-caught seafood
- [ ] Pork shoulder
- [ ] Chicken thighs and drumsticks
- [ ] Italian sausage

Cooking & Preparation Suggestions:

These tools help make your delicious meal preparations and cooking quicker and easier. Especially the cleanup!

Food processor–Kitchenaid
Immersion blender
Parchment paper
Glass meal prep containers with lids–Pyrex
Instapot, Crock-pot or stainless-steel large soup pot
Cast iron or stainless-steel sauté pan–Without Teflon or nonstick coating–All-Clad

Standup blender–Ninja, Kitchenaid, VitaMix
Silicone (BPA-free) muffin liners
Rimmed sheet pan–All-Clad

Shopping Suggestions:

I utilize local organic produce, and grass-fed and finished meat delivery service in my area. This includes an overview of the products they offer, business hours, and acceptable forms of payment accepted. Search for one near you. National Farmers Market Directory is available on their website: ***ams.usda.gov/local-food-directories/farmersmarkets***

Community Supported Agriculture Resources:

- *LocalHarvest.org/csa*
- *HungryHarvest.net*
- *ImperfectProduce.com*

Guides to Grass-Fed Meat:

- Directory of approved producers of grass-fed meat by state from the American Grassfed Association: ***AmericanGrassfed.org/***.
- Directory of pasture-based farms throughout America and includes grass-fed meat, dairy, poultry, and eggs: ***Eatwild.com/products***.
- Resource for local grass-fed beef, poultry, eggs, and produce: ***LocalHarvest.org***.
- EWG has a guide to meat-related labels, certifications, and best practices for the health-conscious meat eater, "Meat Eater's Guide to Climate Change and Health" (***EWG.org/meateatersguide/eat-smart***).
- Resource for locating sustainably raised poultry and eggs: ***EatWellGuide.org***.
- CAFO provides information about the practices of industrial animal agriculture and the risks to public health and the environment, as well as, the mistreatment of the animals: ***CAFOthebook.org.***
- Online companies for organic, grass-fed, and finished meats include Butcher's Box, 5 Mary's, and Moink.

Seafood:

- Read EWG's "Consumer Guide to Seafood" to determine which types of seafood are the safest and which should be avoided: ***EWG.org/research/ewgs-good-seafood-guide***
- This is a handy guide on how to buy fish that is good for you and our environment, "Natural Resources Defense Council" ***https://www.nrdc.org/stories/smart-seafood-buying-guide***
- Lowest mercury seafood: Anchovies, Butterfish, Catfish, Clam, Domestic Crab, Crawfish/Crayfish, Atlantic Croaker, Flounder, Atlantic Haddock, Hake, Herring, Jacksmelt/Silverside, N. Atlantic Mackerel (Chub), Mullet, Oyster, Plaice, Pollock, Canned Salmon, Fresh Salmon, Sardine, Scallop, Shrimp, Pacific Sole, Calamari/Squid, Tilapia, Freshwater Trout, Whitefish, and Whiting.
- A resource to guide you if you plan to eat farmed fish: ***cleanfish.com***

General Shopping Tips:

- National Chain Stores that carry a lot of organic produce include Aldi, Sprouts, Nature's Food Patch, Costco, Whole Foods and local chains like Publix, Wegmans, and Harris Teeter. These stores have been listening to consumer demands for more choices and are starting to carry more organic produce!
- Gluten-free information: ***Celiac.com***
- Non-GMO Project is a comprehensive resource with up-to-date information on non-GMO labeling initiatives and safe product: ***NonGMOProject.org***
- EWG's "Shopper's Guide to Avoiding GMOs," ***EWG.org/research/shoppers-guide-to-avoiding-gmos***
- Dry Farm Wines is a wine club that focuses on biodynamic, additive-free, low-alcohol, and sugar-free wines that are lab tested for purity: ***DryFarmWines.com***

YOUR NOTES

15

Shopping Guides & Produce References

EWG's 2020 "Dirty Dozen"

These produce items contain the highest levels of pesticides, therefore, always purchase these organic: [22]

1. Strawberries
2. Spinach
3. Kale
4. Nectarines
5. Apples
6. Grapes
7. Peaches
8. Cherries
9. Pears
10. Tomatoes
11. Celery
12. Potatoes

Shop for ORGANIC ingredients

> Non-organic hot peppers are treated with neurotoxic pesticides.
> Always purchase these produce items organic.

EWG's 2020 "Clean Fifteen"

Listed are fifteen produce items with the lowest levels of pesticides and if cost or availability is an issue, purchase these items non-organic[21]:

1. Avocados
2. Pineapple
3. Onion
4. Sweet peas
5. Eggplant
6. Asparagus
7. Cauliflower
8. Cantaloupe
9. Broccoli
10. Mushrooms
11. Cabbage
12. Honeydew melon
13. Kiwi
14. Sweet Corn
15. Papaya

Since there is still pesticide residue present on these produce items, always wash them well before consuming.

Be cautious with sweet corn, papaya, and summer squash, including zucchini, as non-organic versions are often genetically modified. Organic is the best option for this list.

Organic Produce References:

Organic Consumers Association provides up-to-date information on organic policy initiative, social and environmental issues and product information.
OrganicConsumers.org

USDA National Organic Program (NOP) provides updates on food labeling and is currently in the process of developing food labeling standards on their website:
ams.usda.gov/rule-regulations/organic

16

Dr. Anya's Quick Health Guide

- Build your meal around plant-based foods, especially vegetables.
- Always purchase grass-fed, organic meats and wild-caught fish.
- Opt for non-bovine dairy or ideally avoid dairy entirely.
- Utilize the EWG's "Dirty Dozen" and "Clean Fifteen" Shopping Guides when selecting produce.
- Shop local farmers markets and buy produce in-season.
- Use fresh herbs as finishers to your meals and to make your own dressings and sauces.
- Snack on organic raw olives, coconut, nuts, and seeds, but be mindful of portion size.
- Select from organic coconut, olive, and avocado oils when cooking and baking. Refer to "How Do I Cook with Healthy Fats and Oils" section for specifics (page 35).
- Drink lots of fresh filtered water daily. Aim for half your body weight in ounces every day.
- If alcohol is consumed, ensure it is organic red or white wine and be mindful to limit consumption to 1-2 glasses/week.
- If caffeine is consumed, select organic coffee or green tea without added refined sugar or cow's dairy. Raw honey can be added if sweetness is desired. Organic nut milk is delicious in coffee.

- If purchasing anything in a can or plastic, ensure the label clearly states "BPA-free".
- Exercise daily. Even a daily 15-minute walk has marvelous health benefits.
- Most people should aim for 7-8 hours of sleep each night. Be sure to put down your electronic devices at least 1 but ideally 2 hours before bedtime.
- Learn how to balance the unnatural stress response through natural techniques like meditation, exercise, and deep breathing.

REFERENCES

1. "Additional Information about High-Intensity Sweeteners Permitted for Use in Food in the United States | FDA." 2018. U.S. Food and Drug Administration. FDA. February 8, 2018.
2. Adkinson RW, Gough RH, Graham R, Yilmaz A. Implications of proposed changes in bulk tank somatic cell count regulations. J Dairy Sci. 2001 Feb;84(2):370-4.
3. Back to Health Functional Medicine. 2020. Back to Health FM. 2020.
4. Basu S., Yoffe P., Hills N., Lustig R.H. The relationship of sugar to population-level diabetes prevalence: An econometric analysis of repeated cross-sectional data. PLoS ONE. 2013;8:e57873.
5. Bartrina J.A., Rodrigo C.P. Association between sucrose intake and cancer: A review of the evidence. Nutr. Hosp. 2013;4:95–105.
6. Bouchard MF, Bellinger DC, Wright RO, Weisskopf MG. Attention-deficit/hyperactivity disorder and urinary metabolites of organophosphate pesticides. Pediatrics. 2010 Jun; 125(6):e1270-7.
7. Bourre JM. Effect of nutrients (in food) on the structure and function of the nervous system: Update on dietary requirements for brain, Part 1: Micronutrients. J Nutr Health Aging. 2006;10:377–85.
8. Bray G.A. Fructose and risk of cardiometabolic disease. Curr. Atheroscler. Rep. 2012;14:570–578.
9. Bray G.A., Popkin B.M. Calorie-sweetened beverages and fructose: What have we learned 10 years later. Pediatr. Obes. 2013;8:242–248.
10. Cantley L.C. Cancer, metabolism, fructose, artificial sweeteners, and going cold turkey on sugar. BMC Biol. 2014;12:8.
11. Carter BD, Abnet CC, Feskanich D, Freedman ND, Hartge P, Lewis CE, et al. Smoking and mortality— beyond established causes. New England Journal of Medicine. 2015;372(7):631–40.
12. Cekici H, Sanlier N. Current nutritional approaches in managing autism spectrum disorder: A review. Nutr Neurosci 2019 Mar;22(3):145-155.
13. Centers for Disease Control and Prevention (CDC) Smoking-attributable mortality, years of potential life lost, and productivity losses--United States, 2000–2004. MMWR Morbidity and mortality weekly report. 2008;57(45):1226–8. Epub 2008/11/15.
14. Clark J.M. The epidemiology of nonalcoholic fatty liver disease in adults. J. Clin. Gastroenterol. 2006;40:S5–S10.
15. Cooking Oils and Smoke Points: What to Know and How to Choose the Right Cooking Oil. Masterclass; Culinary Arts. 2019 Sep 25.
16. Cordain L. Cereal grains: humanity's double-edged sword. World Rev Nutr Diet. 1999; 84:19–73.
17. Cordain L, Eaton SB, Sebastian A et al. Origins and evolution of the western diet: Health implications for the 21st century. Am J Clin Nutr. 2005;81:341-54.
18. Crinnion W. Organic foods contain higher levels of certain nutrients, lower levels of pesticides and may provide health benefits for the consumer. Altern Med Rev. 2010 Apr 15(1):4-12.
19. DiNicolantonio J.J., O'Keefe J.H., Lucan S.C. Added fructose: A principal driver of type 2 diabetes mellitus and its consequences. Mayo Clin. Proc. 2015;90:372–381.
20. Easton MDL, Luszniak D, and E Von der Geest, 2002. Preliminary Examination of Contaminant Loadings in Farmed Salmon, Wild Salmon and Commercial Salmon Feed. Chemosphere (46) 1053-1074.
21. Environmental Working Group. n.d. "EWG's 2020 Shopper's Guide to Pesticides in Produce | Clean

Fifteen." EWG | Environmental Working Group. 2020.
22. Environmental Working Group. n.d. "EWG's 2020 Shopper's Guide to Pesticides in Produce | Dirty Dozen." EWG | Environmental Working Group. 2020.
23. Erskine R. Mastitis in Cattle - Reproductive System - Merck Veterinary Manual. n.d. Merck Veterinary Manual. 2010 May.
24. Fallon, S. Nourishing Traditions: the Cookbook That Challenges Politically Correct Nutrition and the Diet Dictocrats. New Trends Publishing, 2001.
25. Feig D., Soletsky B., Johnson R. Effect of allopurinol on blood pressure of adolescents with newly diagnosed essential hypertension. J. Am. Med. Assoc. 2008;300:924–932.
26. Felton CV, Crook D, Davies MJ, Oliver MF. Dietary polyunsaturated fatty acids and composition of human aortic plaques. Lancet. 1994;344(8931):1195-1196. doi:10.1016/s0140-6736(94)90511-8.
27. "Food Intolerance: Immune Activation Through Diet-Associated Stimuli in Chronic Disease - PubMed." n.d. PubMed.
28. Gaskins A, Chavarro J. Diet and fertility: a review. Am J Obstet Gynecol. 2018 Apr;218(4):379-389
29. Goran M.I., Ulijaszek S.J., Ventura E.E. High fructose corn syrup and diabetes prevalence: A global perspective. Glob. Public Health. 2013;8:55–64.
30. Grant JD. Time for change: Benefits of a plant-based diet. Canadian family physician Medecin de famille canadien.
31. Gurian-Sherman D. CAFOs uncovered. The untold costs of confined animal feeding operations. Cambridge, MA: Union of Concerned Scientists; 2008.
32. Hadjivassiliou M et al. Neuropathy associated with gluten sensitivity. J Neurol Neurosurg Psych. 2006; 77:1262-66.
33. Hall KD, et al. Ultra-processed diets cause excess calorie intake and weight gain: A one-month inpatient randomized controlled trial of ad libitum food intake. Cell Metabolism. May 16, 2019.
34. Health UDo, Human Services. The health consequences of smoking—50 years of progress: a report of the Surgeon General. Atlanta, GA: US Department of Health and Human Services, Centers for Disease Control and Prevention, National Center for Chronic Disease Prevention and Health Promotion, Office on Smoking and Health; 2014. p. 17
35. How to Understand and Use the Nutrition Facts Label | FDA. U.S. Food and Drug Administration. FDA. 2005.
36. IARC Monographs on the Evaluation of Carcinogenic Risks to Humans, No. 95. IARC Working Group on the Evaluation of Carcinogenic Risk to Humans. Lyon (FR): International Agency for Research on Cancer; 2010.
37. Kahleova H, Fleeman R, Hlozkova A, Hlozkova R, Barnard N. A plant-based diet in overweight individuals in a 16-week randomized clinical trial: metabolic benefits of plant protein. Nutr Diabetes. 2018; 8: 58.
38. Kanuckel A. Companion Planting Guide: 10 Veggies That Should Grow Together. Home and Garden. Farmers' Almanac.
39. Krakowiak P, Walker CK, Bremer AA, Baker AS, Ozonoff S, Hansen RL, Hertz-Picciotto I. 2012. Maternal metabolic conditions and risk for autism and other neurodevelopmental disorders. Pediatrics 129(5):e1121-e1128.
40. Lankarani K. Diet and the Gut. Middle East J Dig Dis. 2016 Jul; 8(3): 161-165.
41. Lau, K. Your Plan for Natural Scoliosis Prevention and Treatment: The Ultimate Program and Workbook to a Stronger and Straighter Spine. Health In Your Hands Pte Ltd, 2011
42. Liu A, et al. A healthy approach to dietary fats: understanding the science and taking action to reduce consumer confusion. Nutr J. Aug 30 2017; 16:53.
43. Machpherson AJ, Harris NL. Interactions between commensal intestinal bacteria and the immune system. Nat Rev Immunol. 2004;4:478–85.
44. Malik V.S., Popkin B.M., Bray G.A., Després J.-P., Hu F.B. Sugar-sweetened beverages, obesity, type 2 diabetes mellitus, and cardiovascular disease risk. Circulation. 2010;121:1356–1364.
45. Malik V.S., Schulze M.B., Hu F.B. Intake of sugar-sweetened beverages and weight gain: A systematic review.

Am. J. Clin. Nutr. 2006;84:274–288.

46. Manzel A, et. Al. Role of "Western Diet" in Inflammatory Autoimmune Diseases. Curr Allergy Asthma Rep. 2014 Jan; 14(1); 404.

47. Marckmann P. Dietary treatment of thrombogenic disorders related to the metabolic syndrome. Br. J. Nutr. 2000;83(Suppl. 1):S121–S126.

48. Maurizi CP. The therapeutic potential for tryptophan and melatonin: Possible roles in depression, sleep, Alzheimer's disease and abnormal aging. Med Hypotheses. 1990; 31:233–42.

49. Mazurek R, M Elliott. Seafood Watch, Seafood Report: Farmed Atlantic Salmon. Monterey Bay Aquarium. 2004.

50. McCullough A. Update on nonalcoholic fatty liver disease. J. Clin. Gastroenterol. 2002;34:255–262.

51. Murphy M, Mercer J. Diet-Regulated Anxiety. Int J Endocrinol. 2013; 2013:701967.

52. Murray CJL, Lopez AD. The global burden of disease. World Health Organization. 1996:270; 10. National Center for Health Statistics. National Vital Statistics System: Multiple Cause of Death Data File, 1980–2014. Hyattsville, MD: National Center for Health Statistics; 2014.

53. Ng, S.W., Slining, M.M., & Popkin, B.M. (2012). Use of caloric and noncaloric sweeteners in US consumer packaged foods, 2005-2009. Journal of the Academy of Nutrition and Dietetics, 112(11), 1828-1834.e1821-1826.

54. Nguyen S., Choi H.K., Lustig R.H., Hsu C.Y. Sugar-sweetened beverages, serum uric acid, and blood pressure in adolescents. J. Pediatr. 2009;154:807–813.

55. Nielsen ES, Garnas E, Jensen KJ, Hansen LH, Olsen PS, Ritz C, Krych L, Nielsen DS. Lacto-fermented sauerkraut improves symptoms in IBS patients independent of product pasteurization – a pilot study. Food Funct. 2018 Oct 17;9(10):5323-5335.

56. Olsen N.J., Heitmann B.L. Intake of calorically sweetened beverages and obesity. Obes. Rev. 2009;10:68–75.

57. Pickle W.L., Mungiole M, Jones GK, White AA. Atlas of United States Mortality. Hyattsville, MD: National Center for Health Statistics; 1996.

58. Pelucchi C, Gallus S, Garavello W, Bosetti C, La Vecchia C. Cancer risk associated with alcohol and tobacco use: focus on upper aero-digestive tract and liver. Alcohol Research & Health. 2006;29(3):193–9.

59. Pietschmann N. Food Intolerance: Immune Activation Through Diet-associated Stimuli in Chronic Disease. Altern Ther Health Med. 2015;21(4):42-52.

60. Potterton, D., ed. Culpepper's Color Herbal. New York: Sterling, 1983.

61. Presseau T, Malla S, Klein KK. Health claim regulations on foods: impacts on life expectancy in Canada and the United States. Canadian journal of public health. April 20, 2020.

62. Recombinant Bovine Growth Hormone. 2014. American Cancer Society | Information and Resources about for Cancer: Breast, Colon, Lung, Prostate, Skin. October 9, 2014.

63. Rehm J, Mathers C, Popova S, Thavorncharoensap M, Teerawattananon Y, Patra J. Global burden of disease and injury and economic cost attributable to alcohol use and alcohol-use disorders. The Lancet. 2009;373(9682):2223–33.

64. Ricci A, Bernini V, Maoloni A, Crilini M, Galaverna G, Nevianai E, Lazzi C. Vegetable By-Product Lacto-Fermentation as a New Source of Antimicrobial Compounds. Microorganisms. 2019 Nov 22;7(12).

65. Rosengren A, Wilhelmsen L, Wedel H. Separate and Combined Effects of Smoking and Alcohol Abuse in Middle-aged Men. Acta Medica Scandinavica. 1988;223(2):111–8.

66. Ryan-Harshman M, Aldoori W. How diet and lifestyle affect duodenal ulcers. Review of the evidence. Can Fam Physician. 2004 May; 50:727-732.

67. Sales-Campos H., Reis de Souza P., Peghini B.C., et al. An Overview of the Modulatory Effects of Oleic Acid in Health and Disease. Mini Rev Med Chem. 2013 Feb;13(2):201-10.

68. Sathyanarayana Rao T. S., Asha M. R., Ramesh B. N., and Jagannatha Rao K. S.. Understanding nutrition, depression and mental illnesses. Indian J Psychiatry. 2008 Apr-Jun; 50(2): 77–82.

69. Schramm, Derek D. You Only Weigh 10 Pounds on the Moon: Lessons for Being an Active Participant in Your Shape, Weight, and Longevity. Derek D. Schramm, 2018.
70. Schmidt RJ, Hansen RL, Hartiala J, Allayee H, Schmidt LC, Tancredi DJ, Tassone F, Hertz-Picciotto I. 2011. Prenatal vitamins, one-carbon metabolism gene variants, and risk for autism. Epidemiology 22(4):476-485.
71. Schwalfenberg G. The Alkaline Diet: Is There Evidence That an Alkaline pH Diet Benefits Health? J Environ Public Health 2012; 2012:727630)
72. Seaman DR. Nutritional considerations for inflammation and pain. In: Liebenson CL. Editor. Rehabilitation of the spine: a practitioners manual. 2nd ed.; 2006: p.728-740
73. Seaman, David R. The Deflame Diet: Deflame Your Diet, Body, and Mind. Shadow Panther Press, 2016.
74. Seaman DR. The diet-induced pro-inflammatory state: a cause of chronic pain and other degenerative diseases? J Manipulative Physiol Ther. 2002; 25(3):168-79.
75. Shively CA, Appt SE, Vitolins MZ, et al. Mediterranean versus Western Diet Effects on Caloric Intake, Obesity, Metabolism, and Hepatosteatosis in Nonhuman Primates. Obesity May 2019.
76. Sigman-Grant, M., & Morita, J. (2003, October). Defining and interpreting intakes of sugars. The American Journal of Clinical Nutrition, 78(4), 815S-826S. doi:PMID: 14522745.
77. Simon, David Robinson. 2020. "7 Things Everyone Should Know About Farmed Fish." Mindbodygreen. March 25, 2020.
78. Song P., Wu L., Guan W. Dietary Nitrates, Nitrites, and Nitrosamines Intake and the Risk of Gastric Cancer: A Meta-Analysis. Nutrients. 2015 Dec 1;7(12):9872-95.
79. Stanhope KL. Sugar consumption, metabolic disease and obesity: The state of the controversy. Crit Rev Clin Lab Sci 2016;53(1):52-67.
80. Stephan B.C., Wells J.C., Brayne C., Albanese E., Siervo M. Increased fructose intake as a risk factor for dementia. J. Gerontol. A. Biol. Sci. Med. Sci. 2010;65:809–814.
81. SugarScience | Hidden in Plain Sight. 2013. SugarScience.UCSF.Edu. November 17, 2013.
82. The Dairy Industry | PETA. 2010. PETA. June 22, 2010.
83. Thomas S, Browne H, Mobasheri A, Rayman M. What is the evidence for a role for diet and nutrition in osteoarthritis? Rheumatology (Oxford). 2018 May; 57; iv61-iv74.
84. Trogdon JG, Murphy LB, Khavjou OA, et al. Costs of Chronic Diseases at the State Level: The Chronic Disease Cost Calculator. Preventing chronic disease. September 3, 2015.
85. "Understanding Food Labels | Food & Water Watch." 2018. Food & Water Watch. July 12, 2018.
86. Waknitz FW, Iwamoto RN, and MS Strom, 2003. Interactions of Atlantic salmon in the Pacific Northwest. IV. Impacts on the local Ecosystems. Fisheries Research 62 (2003) 307-328.
87. Weaver C. Diet, Gut Microbiome and Bone Health. Curr Osteoporos Rep. 2015 Apr; 13(2); 125-130.
88. Weaver KL et al. The content of favorable and unfavorable polyunsaturated fatty acids found in commonly eaten fish. J Am Diet Assoc. 2008; 108(7):1178-85
89. Wells AS, Read NW, Laugharne JD, Ahluwalia NS. Alterations in mood after changing to a low-fat diet. Br J Nutr. 1998;79(1):23-30.
90. Zheng T, Boyle P, Zhang B, Zhang Y, Owens PH, Lan Q. Tobacco use and risk of oral cancer. Tobacco: Science, Policy and Public Health; 2004. pp. 399–432.

Made in the USA
Columbia, SC
23 February 2023